W9-BRA-756

OPPOSING
VIEWPOINTS®
SERIES

Child Custody

Other Books of Related Interest:

Opposing Viewpoints Series

Juvenile Crime

Teens and Employment

Welfare

At Issue Series

Do Students Have Too Much Homework?

Should Juveniles Be Given Life Without Parole?

Current Controversies Series

America's Teachers

Teens and Privacy

"Congress shall make no law ... abridging the freedom of speech, or of the press."

First Amendment to the U.S. Constitution

The basic foundation of our democracy is the First Amendment guarantee of freedom of expression. The *Opposing Viewpoints* series is dedicated to the concept of this basic freedom and the idea that it is more important to practice it than to enshrine it.

OPPOSING VIEWPOINTS® SERIES

| Child Custody

Dedria Bryfonski, Book Editor

GREENHAVEN PRESS
A part of Gale, Cengage Learning

CABARRUS COUNTY PUBLIC LIBRARY
HARRISBURG LIBRARY
HARRISBURG, NORTH CAROLINA 28075

GALE
CENGAGE Learning™

Detroit • New York • San Francisco • New Haven, Conn • Waterville, Maine • London

3 3083 00614 5251

Christine Nasso, *Publisher*
Elizabeth Des Chenes, *Managing Editor*

© 2011 Greenhaven Press, a part of Gale, Cengage Learning

Gale and Greenhaven Press are registered trademarks used herein under license.

For more information, contact:
Greenhaven Press
27500 Drake Rd.
Farmington Hills, MI 48331-3535
Or you can visit our Internet site at gale.cengage.com

ALL RIGHTS RESERVED.
No part of this work covered by the copyright herein may be reproduced, transmitted, stored, or used in any form or by any means graphic, electronic, or mechanical, including but not limited to photocopying, recording, scanning, digitizing, taping, Web distribution, information networks, or information storage and retrieval systems, except as permitted under Section 107 or 108 of the 1976 United States Copyright Act, without the prior written permission of the publisher.

For product information and technology assistance, contact us at

Gale Customer Support, 1-800-877-4253
For permission to use material from this text or product, submit all requests online at www.cengage.com/permissions

Further permissions questions can be emailed to permissionrequest@cengage.com

Articles in Greenhaven Press anthologies are often edited for length to meet page requirements. In addition, original titles of these works are changed to clearly present the main thesis and to explicitly indicate the author's opinion. Every effort is made to ensure that Greenhaven Press accurately reflects the original intent of the authors. Every effort has been made to trace the owners of copyrighted material.

Cover image copyright © iStockPhoto.com/spxChrome.

LIBRARY OF CONGRESS CATALOGING-IN-PUBLICATION DATA

Child custody / Dedria Bryfonski, book editor.
    p. cm. -- (Opposing viewpoints)
    Includes bibliographical references and index.
    ISBN 978-0-7377-5217-5 (hbk.) -- ISBN 978-0-7377-5218-2 (pbk.)
    1. Custody of children--United States--Juvenile literature. 2. Custodial parents--United States--Juvenile literature. 3. Children's rights--United States--Juvenile literature. I. Bryfonski, Dedria.
    HV715.C534 2011
    346.7301'73--dc22

                                        2010037584

Printed in the United States of America
1 2 3 4 5 6 7 15 14 13 12 11

Contents

Chapter 2: How Should Custody Be Determined for Adopted Children?

Chapter 3: What Is the Role of Government in Determining Child Custody?

Chapter 4: Should Abduction Be Used in International Custody Disputes?

Why Consider Opposing Viewpoints?

> *"The only way in which a human being can make some approach to knowing the whole of a subject is by hearing what can be said about it by persons of every variety of opinion and studying all modes in which it can be looked at by every character of mind. No wise man ever acquired his wisdom in any mode but this."*
>
> *John Stuart Mill*

In our media-intensive culture it is not difficult to find differing opinions. Thousands of newspapers and magazines and dozens of radio and television talk shows resound with differing points of view. The difficulty lies in deciding which opinion to agree with and which "experts" seem the most credible. The more inundated we become with differing opinions and claims, the more essential it is to hone critical reading and thinking skills to evaluate these ideas. Opposing Viewpoints books address this problem directly by presenting stimulating debates that can be used to enhance and teach these skills. The varied opinions contained in each book examine many different aspects of a single issue. While examining these conveniently edited opposing views, readers can develop critical thinking skills such as the ability to compare and contrast authors' credibility, facts, argumentation styles, use of persuasive techniques, and other stylistic tools. In short, the Opposing Viewpoints Series is an ideal way to attain the higher-level thinking and reading skills so essential in a culture of diverse and contradictory opinions.

In addition to providing a tool for critical thinking, *Opposing Viewpoints* books challenge readers to question their own strongly held opinions and assumptions. Most people form their opinions on the basis of upbringing, peer pressure, and personal, cultural, or professional bias. By reading carefully balanced opposing views, readers must directly confront new ideas as well as the opinions of those with whom they disagree. This is not to argue simplistically that everyone who reads opposing views will—or should—change his or her opinion. Instead, the series enhances readers' understanding of their own views by encouraging confrontation with opposing ideas. Careful examination of others' views can lead to the readers' understanding of the logical inconsistencies in their own opinions, perspective on why they hold an opinion, and the consideration of the possibility that their opinion requires further evaluation.

Evaluating Other Opinions

To ensure that this type of examination occurs, *Opposing Viewpoints* books present all types of opinions. Prominent spokespeople on different sides of each issue as well as well-known professionals from many disciplines challenge the reader. An additional goal of the series is to provide a forum for other, less known, or even unpopular viewpoints. The opinion of an ordinary person who has had to make the decision to cut off life support from a terminally ill relative, for example, may be just as valuable and provide just as much insight as a medical ethicist's professional opinion. The editors have two additional purposes in including these less known views. One, the editors encourage readers to respect others' opinions—even when not enhanced by professional credibility. It is only by reading or listening to and objectively evaluating others' ideas that one can determine whether they are worthy of consideration. Two, the inclusion of such viewpoints encourages the important critical thinking skill of objectively evaluating an author's credentials and bias. This evaluation will illuminate an author's reasons for taking a particular stance on an issue and will aid in readers' evaluation of the author's ideas.

It is our hope that these books will give readers a deeper understanding of the issues debated and an appreciation of the complexity of even seemingly simple issues when good and honest people disagree. This awareness is particularly important in a democratic society such as ours in which people enter into public debate to determine the common good. Those with whom one disagrees should not be regarded as enemies but rather as people whose views deserve careful examination and may shed light on one's own.

Thomas Jefferson once said that "difference of opinion leads to inquiry, and inquiry to truth." Jefferson, a broadly educated man, argued that "if a nation expects to be ignorant and free . . . it expects what never was and never will be." As individuals and as a nation, it is imperative that we consider the opinions of others and examine them with skill and discernment. The *Opposing Viewpoints* Series is intended to help readers achieve this goal.

David L. Bender and Bruno Leone,
Founders

Introduction

"The only clearly discernible thread that weaves through the complex patterns of the past is that the role and legal status of women has had the most impact on custody arrangements in the past."

Mary Ann Mason,
From Father's Property
to Children's Rights:
The History of Child Custody
in the United States, *1994*

Child custody cases in the news, the most complex of which sometimes involve issues such as international abduction, surrogate parenthood, and the parental rights of non-biological gay partners, demonstrate the difficulty of determining custody in an age of changing social and political conditions. In addition to becoming increasingly complex, child custody deliberations are also becoming far more widespread. As of 2010, it was estimated that more than one-half of all children will be subject to a child custody determination before they reach age eighteen. One out of every two children will live in a single-parent home at some point before reaching age eighteen. In 2007, for example, 32 percent lived in a one-parent home. The number of children living with one parent has tripled since 1970, as divorce has become more commonplace.

As the number of children affected by child custody determinations has skyrocketed over the years, the criteria to determine custody have also undergone sweeping changes. A look at this history of child custody reveals that changes are made to laws and customs to reflect changes in society.

From colonial times up until the middle of the nineteenth century, the practice of English common law, which granted child custody to fathers, was the rule in the United States. During this time, women had no legal status, including no rights to their own children. Additionally, during this time children were more valued for their potential economic contribution than for their emotional contribution to a family, and thus were deemed the property of the father. Because divorce was a relatively rare occurrence, questions of child custody were most commonly raised when children were left orphans or otherwise came under the care of the state.

By the latter part of the nineteenth century, with waves of immigrants coming to the United States seeking jobs, child labor became less common and less important economically to the family. A higher value was placed on educating and nurturing children, and mothers assumed the primary responsibility for these roles. The need of the child for the nurture and stability of a primary parent became the legal standard determining custody under a doctrine known as "tender years." Because mothers were the primary caregivers for their children in most households, courts favored awarding custody to them, except in cases where the mother was clearly unfit or unable to perform the duties of parenthood.

The social upheaval of the 1960s made divorce more common. The feminist movement and large numbers of women joining the workforce led to a questioning of the validity of traditional gender roles. In this environment, child custody practices again changed. By the mid-1970s, the "best interests of the child" doctrine replaced the "tender years" doctrine, and child custody cases were determined less on the gender of the parent and more on the needs of the child. While best-interest factors vary from state to state, according to the Child Welfare Information Gateway, the most common factors include:

- The emotional ties and relationship between the child and his or her parents, siblings, family, and household members, or other caregivers;

- The capacity of the parents to provide a safe home and adequate food, clothing, and medical care;

- The mental and physical health needs of the child;

- The mental and physical health of the parents;

- The absence of domestic violence in the home.

Additionally, a number of states require courts to consider the child's wishes when determining custody.

Regardless of the changes in the law, the legal system has been slow to catch up with changing family situations. Specifically, modern-day social and cultural changes have made it more difficult to determine precisely what is in a child's best interests. Consider the following cases:

Elizabet Rodriguez and her boyfriend were determined to escape Cuba with her five-year-old son, Elián González, seeking refuge in Florida. They fled by sea in November 1999, but the boat they and others were sailing in capsized. Both the mother and boyfriend drowned, and Elián was one of only three survivors. His rescue set off an international custody dispute. Juan Miguel González, Elián's father, claimed his son had been kidnapped by his ex-wife and asked that the boy be returned to him in Cuba. Elián's paternal relatives in Miami contended that Elián's mother had died in an attempt to have her son raised in freedom, and therefore, he should remain in their custody in Florida. After the U.S. Immigration and Naturalization Service placed Elián with his Miami relatives, the father petitioned for asylum for his son, and the courts upheld his request. Following a dramatic raid on the relatives' home in Miami, Elián and his father were reunited in June 2000.

Mary Beth Whitehead contracted to become surrogate mother to a child for William and Elizabeth Stern. She was artificially inseminated with William Stern's sperm, and she delivered a baby in March 1986. After giving the baby to the Sterns, Whitehead changed her mind and regained physical custody of the child, who became known as "Baby M." The Sterns sued for custody and won, with the courts citing the "best interests of the child" doctrine. A later court ruling granted Whitehead visitation rights.

A lesbian couple, Janet Jenkins and Lisa Miller, were married in a civil union in Vermont in 2000. Miller was artificially inseminated and gave birth to Isabella Jenkins-Miller in 2002. By 2004, Miller became a born-again Christian and decided she was no longer a lesbian. The couple dissolved their civil union. Miller moved from Vermont to Virginia, where she sought sole custody of Isabella. The Virginia courts initially agreed with her, because the state, unlike Vermont, didn't recognize parental rights in a same-sex civil union. Jenkins continued to fight in court, winning visitation rights in a Vermont court, and eventually having those rights upheld in the Virginia court system. When Miller failed to comply, Jenkins was granted physical custody of Isabella. As of June 2010, the former partners were still fighting over Isabella's custody.

As the cases cited above demonstrate, the traditional family of the 1970s and before has given way to a new family structure that often results in unique complications during child custody determinations. In the viewpoints that follow, sociologists, psychologists, commentators, and journalists offer varying opinions on child custody in four chapters that ask: How Should Custody Be Determined When Parents Divorce? How Should Custody Be Determined for Adopted Children? What Is the Role of Government in Determining Child Custody? and Should Abduction Be Used in International Custody Disputes? The varying viewpoints in *Opposing View-*

points: Child Custody give the reader some idea of the complexity and difficulty of the issues surrounding child custody in the new millennium.

OPPOSING
VIEWPOINTS®
SERIES

How Should Custody Be Determined When Parents Divorce?

Chapter Preface

Despite a society that is becoming more gender neutral and the activism of men's rights groups, in 2008 the National Center for Health Statistics estimated that fathers were granted sole physical custody of their children in only 10 percent of divorces, with mothers getting custody 75 percent of the time and joint custody or custody by a non-parent the other 15 percent. Although the "best interests of the child" doctrine is the standard to determine custody, in the vast majority of cases, courts rule it is in a child's best interests for the mother to have sole physical custody.

Even so, cases such as the custody battle between pop superstar Britney Spears and her actor-dancer-rapper ex-husband Kevin Federline demonstrate some of the reasons why a court will award custody of even very young children to a father. Spears and Federline were married in September 2004, and within the course of two years, the couple produced two sons. In November 2006, Spears filed for divorce, and both Spears and Federline sought sole physical custody of the boys with visitation rights for the other parent. After a lengthy and bitter dispute, the pair agreed to joint physical custody in March 2007.

The months that followed saw Spears in the headlines on multiple occasions for actions that put into question her fitness to be a mother. Excessive partying, careless driving, actions that endangered the safety of her children, and suspected drug and alcohol abuse led to court appearances by Spears, and she was eventually hospitalized. Federline sued for sole custody and was awarded it in October 2007, making Spears the rare celebrity mom who loses custody of her children. As of June 2010, Federline retained sole custody of the children, with Spears having gradually gained visitation rights.

Another bitter celebrity custody battle brought attention to the ways in which the court system can be manipulated to challenge a custody determination. Actors Alec Baldwin and Kim Basinger divorced in 2002 after nine years of marriage, and the couple became engaged in a bitter custody battle for their only child, daughter Ireland. The battle went on for eight years, cost $3 million in legal fees, and resulted in ninety-one court proceedings. Each called the other an unfit parent, with Baldwin alleging that Basinger was mentally unstable, and Basinger alleging that Baldwin was emotionally abusive. Although a court ruled in 2004 that custody be shared between the parents, the couple continued their legal battle. According to Baldwin, Basinger turned her daughter against him and created obstacles to him being able to have access to his child. According to Basinger, Baldwin needed to deal with issues such as anger management before being allowed access to Ireland. In September 2007, the case gained notoriety when a frustrated Baldwin left a voice message for Ireland in which he called her "a rude, thoughtless little pig." The message was leaked to the press and caused Baldwin to temporarily lose access to his daughter. The case has been used to illustrate the failures of a court system that permits such drawn-out custody battles.

Since the early 1970s, the legal standard being upheld in custody cases resulting from divorce has been the best interests of the child. But as society becomes increasingly complex, how do courts weigh conflicting interests to determine what is truly in a child's best interest? In the viewpoints contained in the following chapter, commentators offer differing opinions on how custody should be determined when parents divorce.

> "With joint custody, the child is entitled to spend at least a third to half of the time on a year-round basis with each parent."

Joint Custody Is the Best Solution

David Levy

David Levy is a lawyer and the chief executive officer of the Children's Rights Council, a global child advocacy organization located in Landover, Maryland.

In approximately one out of every ten thousand cases, custody battles end in violence, with children being injured or killed. In many of these cases, one parent or both are attempting to gain sole custody of the child or children, according to Levy in the following viewpoint. Because violent behavior is almost impossible to predict, it is more prudent to seek an arrangement that gives each parent equal access. Under joint custody arrangements, children experience more normal relationships with both parents, Levy contends.

As you read, consider the following questions:

1. What are common characteristics of sole custody cases?

David Levy, "Shared Parenting Is Better than Sole Custody," *Policy & Practice*, vol. 66, June 2008, p. 26. Copyright © 2008 APHSA. All rights reserved. Reproduced by permission.

2. According to the author, what is one of the benefits to the child of joint custody?

3. What is the role of the access centers operated by the Children's Rights Council in custody arrangements?

The headlines tell it all: a father shoots his three children, his ex-wife, then kills himself in the middle of a custody dispute; a mother drowns her children by driving them in a car into a lake; a father kills his three children, then tries to kill himself with pills, but his suicide attempt backfires, and he is arrested and will stand trial for the murder of his children.

Bitter Sole Custody Battles Can Result in Tragedy

Actually, the headlines do not tell it all. They only relate the final, horrible tragedy of cases that occur around the country with depressing regularity. It is difficult to step back and assess the context of these cases within the overall custody system, but it is about time we do so.

Aside from considering the mental illness of a parent who would kill his children, we need to examine the circumstances in which these awful cases occur, rather than the usual reaction that the courts should have kept these parents from their children. It is difficult to know beforehand which one out of 10,000 cases will erupt so disastrously.

We do know that these tragedies are tied to bitter custody battles. These are almost always sole custody battles, in which each parent is fighting to be the dominant, primary force in the lives of their children after the divorce.

The common characteristics of these sole custody cases is that each parent works to picture herself or himself as the better parent, and even at the cost of going bankrupt, a parent will spend thousands on lawyers and expert witnesses to show the court why she or he is entitled to sole custody. The battles can continue for months or years, and the emotional and psychological effects on the family grow more attenuated the longer the battle continues.

Most states and the District of Columbia have found a way around this custody warfare. They have established a presumption or preference for joint custody, also known as shared parenting. With joint custody, the child is entitled to spend at least a third to half of the time on a year-round basis with each parent. Various arrangements are possible to suit the needs of divorced, separated or never-married parents. The result is that each parent will continue to be an integral part of the child's life, so there is less need for struggle and conflict.

Thirteen states have no statutory language promoting shared parenting. They are Hawaii, Indiana, Maryland, Nebraska, New Jersey, New York, North Carolina, North Dakota, Rhode Island, South Carolina, South Dakota, Utah and Wyoming. In these states, it is virtually impossible for a child to obtain frequent contact with both his or her mother *and* father post-divorce. But if states encourage the child to be able to interact with both parents, most family situations will work out satisfactorily. Not perfectly—but sufficiently amenable to allow most children fairly normal comings and goings with their moms *and* dads, as the states that encourage shared parenting have learned.

It Is Impossible to Predict Violent Behavior

The comment one might immediately ask is, "You mean you would have given joint custody to the parents who have killed or attempted to kill their children?" Of course not. If I could predict what these parents would do, I would order absolutely no contact between parent and child, and the parents ordered into psychiatric evaluation. Protecting the children comes first.

But the point is that sole custody battles often drive mothers and fathers, pardon the expression, "nuts," especially if they were mentally challenged to begin with. And violence

"Great news Roger . . . ," by Fran, www.CartoonStock.com.

can't be predicted scientifically. Courts need to provide more psychological evaluations in contentious divorces, coupled with mediation, counseling, and parent education. And courts need to step up their use of and funding for access centers, which are operated by the Children's Rights Council and other organization around the country.

These centers offer a safe, secure way to transfer children between parents and provide supervised access when necessary—to prevent a parent from taking the child from the premises until serious issues can be investigated. Under supervised access, a parent and child spend perhaps three or four hours together every week or two in a controlled situation.

Would all of these measures stop those murders of children? There is no way to tell, but an ounce of prevention is worth a pound of cure, as our grandparents used to say, and we need broad reform, not just knee-jerk reactions.

> *"Parents should think long and hard about the short- and long-term challenges of shared parenting for their children and themselves."*

Joint Custody Is Not the Best Solution

Nicki Bradley

Nicki Bradley is a blogger for Families.com.

Although shared custody of children sounds good in theory, in practice there are many issues, states Bradley in the following viewpoint. From the perspective of the child, consistency is important; and it is unsettling for many children to be shuttled from one home to another. As a child reaches the teen years, peer relationships take on increased importance, and taking time away from friends and school activities to spend time with a parent can be disruptive.

As you read, consider the following questions:

1. What are some of the reasons the author gives why parents agree to shared custody?

Nicki Bradley, "The Case Against Joint Physical Custody," Families.com, March 13, 2006, © 2010 Families.com, LLC. Reproduced by permission.

2. How does divorce affect and change parenting style? What are some of the issues that this can cause for joint custody, according to the author?

3. How does remarriage impact custody and parenting arrangements?

We've come a long way since we were children and mothers were routinely given full custody of the children and fathers frequently disappeared and less frequently received a standard visitation schedule of every other weekend visits. In fact, we've come so far that now many courts don't call it "visitation" but more aptly, "parenting time."

We have seen the damage done to children raised without male role models. We have learned our lessons. Now we believe that any child deserves to share as much time as possible with both parents, if they are willing. Most courts will now consider a joint physical custody request and many states will now grant it barring any information presented that would make this sort of arrangement unhealthy for the children.

Although a child's need for a healthy relationship with BOTH parents can't be denied, I believe the extreme turn toward promoting shared custody of children is yet another trend with unforeseen consequences to children and families alike.

Because of the newer popularity of these arrangements, I know more and more families who share custody. Of all the families I know, none are truly satisfied and most have an extremely unhealthy family dynamic. I am sure cases exist where both parents and all involved children are very satisfied; however I think this is the exception rather than the rule unfortunately.

So What Has Gone Wrong?

In theory, joint custody sounds terrific. The children get the best of both worlds, time with both parents. They grow up without any of the trauma associated with divorce because they remain in frequent contact with both parents who interact as a solid co-parenting unit, just like in an intact family.

The problem is the reality rarely looks like this. The reality is that many parents are simply "settling" for shared custody because they fear the money, time and emotional energy they would lose in a full custody fight. Some parents consider the way their ex-spouse parented within the marriage to be of little consequence and don't foresee any problems with sharing. Many parents consider their own needs and the benefits of shared parenting on their own schedules, logistically. This can be a huge motivation for newly single parents to share custody. Raising kids alone is hard work. Sharing the responsibilities is certainly appealing.

But then reality sets in for many of these parents and their children. Some children truly thrive on consistency and often the only type of consistency available in a shared custody arrangement is the consistency that nothing will be consistent! As children grow, their needs change and they have more and more need to develop roots within their community. It can be difficult or impossible for a child to feel settled when their physical environment is changing all the time. When kids become teens, their social network can become seemingly more important than their familial network and being taken away from sports, activities and friends to spend equal time in another environment will often not work at all. Those are all factors that most parents can't control unless they live in the same area as each other.

Shared Parenting Causes Multiple Problems

But there are problems that even parents who are neighbors often can't avoid. It is not unusual for divorced parents to "come out of their shell," to change and alter how they parent their children without the influence of another adult to take into consideration. Shared parenting situations require that both parents continue to take into consideration each other's needs, concerns and opinions and work together. When one or both single parents try to "grow into their own" as single parents, working together can seem impossible. You might find that many of the areas you used to agree on are no longer areas of agreement. You might find values and standards that you took for granted within the marriage are nothing like you thought they would be. You might find that one parent or both are too busy or too tired to enforce the rules or communicate the rules between the households. Disciplinary consistency is almost impossible in joint custody homes.

Many of the same conflicts that existed during the marriage and led to divorce will be present, often at even higher levels, in the post-divorce relationship. How you split expenses and child support can be simple in shared custody situations, or it can be excruciating.

When one or both parents remarry, the opportunity for problems grows exponentially. Now, not only are you trying to continue to peacefully and respectfully co-parent between two parents who could not even get along well enough to remain married but add in one or two additional new parents to the mix who bring with them their own expectations, values, interests, concerns and opinions. Parents who managed to peacefully co-parent before are often taken aback completely when the other parent remarries and suddenly changes in many ways.

Last, but certainly not least, there is the baggage. Like it or not, both women and men often carry emotional baggage that they have yet to heal from their divorce. This baggage all too often is transferred onto the kids. All of the all-too-common mistakes made in "Top 12 Divorced Parenting Mistakes" still appear in shared parenting situations, quite often. And when they do, the consequences can be heightened as the opportunity for conflict, alienation, putting children in the middle, emotionally inappropriate parenting and lack of discipline grow with the frequency of transferring kids between homes.

Parents should think long and hard about the short- and long-term challenges of shared parenting for their children and themselves. Every relationship is different and unique and brings with it challenges that some may be able to work through and others simply won't. Shared parenting shouldn't ever be entered into as a compromise for parents who both want full custody. Instead it should always be entered into as a choice made for the children who deserve as much time as possible with both parents.

> "In study after study, the offspring of lesbian and gay parents have been found to be at least as well adjusted overall as those of other parents."

Gay Parents Should Have Equal Rights in Child Custody Cases

Charlotte J. Patterson

Charlotte J. Patterson teaches in the Department of Psychology of the University of Virginia and is a Williams Distinguished Research Fellow in the School of Law of the University of California, Los Angeles.

In the following viewpoint, Patterson summarizes the research surrounding three main concerns raised by those opposed to gays and lesbians raising children. These concerns are that a child's gender identity may be compromised, personal development may be impaired, and social relationships with peers may suffer. But the results are very clear, Patterson contends. The children of gays and lesbians are as well adjusted as the children of heterosexuals.

Charlotte J. Patterson, "Children of Lesbian and Gay Parents: Psychology, Law, and Policy," *American Psychologist*, vol. 64, November 2009. Copyright © 2009 by the American Psychological Association. Reproduced by permission of the publisher and author.

As you read, consider the following questions:

1. What are some of the activities the author cites to support her contention that there are no differences in gender identity development between children raised by gays and lesbians and those raised by heterosexuals?

2. What are some of the social difficulties the author cites to support her contention that there is no difference in personal development between children raised by gays and lesbians and those raised by heterosexuals?

3. What conclusion does the author reach about the potential for teasing or peer harassment of the children of lesbian mothers?

It has sometimes been suggested that gender development may be compromised among children reared by lesbian or gay parents. Those who express this concern may worry about the development of gender identity (i.e., the fundamental sense of oneself as male or female), about the development of gendered behavior (i.e., the acquisition of behavior that conforms to prevailing norms for masculine or feminine behavior), and/or about the development of sexual orientation (i.e., a person's choice of sexual partners, whether homosexual, heterosexual, or bisexual). To examine the possibilities in this area, researchers have focused their studies on all three of these aspects of gender development.

Research Finds No Gender Identity Issues

The study of gender development and sexual orientation among the offspring of lesbian and gay parents can be criticized on the grounds that atypical gender development and/or nonheterosexuality are neither illnesses nor disabilities. The APA [American Psychological Association] and the American Psychiatric Association, among others, have long disavowed notions of homosexuality or nonnormative gender behavior as representing either disease or disorder. Demands for children to embody heterosexuality or demonstrate only gender behavior that conforms to familiar norms are inappropriate and unwarranted. Nevertheless, such demands are still made in many circles, and they may be especially relevant in child custody cases involving lesbian and gay parents. As a result, researchers have addressed these questions.

It is interesting that research has generally failed to identify important differences in the development of gender identity or gender role behavior as a function of parental sexual orientation. For example, in interviews with children who had grown up with divorced lesbian mothers and children who had grown up with divorced heterosexual mothers, [Richard] Green and his colleagues [in "Lesbian Mothers and Their Children: A Comparison with Solo Parent Heterosexual Mothers and Their Children"] reported no differences with respect to favorite television programs, television characters, games, or toys. [A. Brewaeys, I. Ponjaert, E.V. Van Hall and S. Golombok in "Donor Insemination: Child Development and Family Functioning in Lesbian Mother Families"] used the Pre-School Activities Inventory—a parental report questionnaire designed to assess children's preferences for gendered games, toys, and activities—to assess gender development among children conceived via donor insemination and reared by lesbian or heterosexual couples and reported no significant differences as a function of parental sexual orientation. Using the same instrument, [Charlotte J. Patterson, Rachel H. Farr and Stephen L. Forssell] found no significant differences in the gender role behavior of young children adopted by lesbian, gay, and heterosexual couples. No reports of differences in gender identity as a function of parental sexual orientation have emerged.

A number of researchers have also studied the sexual orientation of those reared by lesbian or gay parents. For instance, [Sharon L.] Huggins interviewed a group of adolescents, half of whom were the offspring of heterosexual mothers and half of whom were the offspring of lesbian mothers. She found that none of the adolescents with lesbian mothers identified as nonheterosexual, but one child of a heterosexual mother did. [Fiona L.] Tasker and [Susan] Golombok also studied the sexual identities of young adults who had been reared by divorced lesbian or divorced heterosexual mothers and reported no differences. [J. Michael Bailey, David Bobrow, Marilyn Wolfe, and Sarah Mikach] interviewed gay fathers about the sexual identities of their adult sons; they found that 7 of 75—9%—of the sons were identified as gay or bisexual. No information about the daughters of these gay fathers was obtained in this study. Overall, the clearest conclusion from these and related studies is that the great majority of children with lesbian or gay parents grow up to identify as heterosexual.

Children's Personal Development Is Not Compromised

A general concern about children of lesbian and gay parents that has been mentioned in many legal and policy debates in the United States is the fear that their personal development might be impaired or compromised. Research has assessed a broad array of characteristics, including separation-individuation, psychiatric evaluations, behavior problems and competencies, self-concept, locus of control, moral judgment, school adjustment, intelligence, victimization, and substance use. As was the case for sexual identity, studies of these aspects of personal development have revealed no major differences between the offspring of lesbian or gay parents and those of heterosexual parents. The research findings thus suggest that concern about difficulties in these areas among the offspring of lesbian mothers is unwarranted.

Particular worries have sometimes been voiced for the development of adolescents with lesbian or gay parents, who are seen as possibly experiencing greater difficulties than younger

Sexual Preference Is Irrelevant

I believe that a truly child-focused analysis leads to the clear conclusion that an adult's sexual orientation generally is irrelevant with respect to placement decisions. Children need homes where they are wanted and receive love and steady care, qualities that are not related to the adult's sexual orientation. Consideration of sexual orientation in placement decisions is likely to be harmful to children. All of the evidence supports this conclusion.

Unfortunately, the interests of children often get lost in debates that really are about adults' visions of the good society. . . . But ultimately, policy rest on values, not data. Social science can inform, but not resolve, policy debates. Policy makers are more likely to look at public attitudes than social science. As public attitudes towards lesbians and gay men have become more positive, so have the policies of courts and legislatures. Hopefully, this trend will continue. Both children and gay adults will be the beneficiaries.

Michael S. Wald,
"Adults' Sexual Orientation and State
Determination Regarding Placement of Children,"
Family Law Quarterly, *Fall 2006.*

children do. In a recent pair of studies, [Jennifer L.] Wainright and colleagues have studied adjustment in a national sample of teenagers in the United States. Their data showed that adolescents living with female same-sex couples did not differ significantly from those living with different-sex couples on measures of anxiety, depressive symptoms, self-esteem, delinquency, or victimization or in their use of tobacco, alcohol, or marijuana. In this nationally representative sample [in Charlotte J. Patterson's "Children of Lesbian and Gay Parents"], whether adolescents' parents had same-sex or different-sex partners was unrelated to adolescent adjustment. Overall, the adjustment of children and adolescents does not appear to be related to parental sexual orientation.

Children's Social Relationships Are Normal

A third type of concern that has been voiced about children and adolescents with lesbian or gay parents is that their social relationships, especially those with peers, may be compromised. To the contrary, however, research has repeatedly found that children and adolescents with nonheterosexual parents report normal social relationships with family members, with peers, and with adults outside their nuclear families. Moreover, observers outside the family agree with these assessments. In particular, the contacts that children of nonheterosexual parents have with extended family members have not been found to differ significantly from those of other children.

Youngsters growing up with lesbian or gay parents have often provided anecdotal reports of teasing or peer harassment that focuses on parental sexual orientation. For instance, [Nanette] Gartrell and her colleagues have reported that a substantial minority of children with lesbian mothers in their longitudinal study reported hearing negative comments from peers. In that most children are probably teased about something, an important question has been the degree to which any such teasing or peer harassment may affect overall adjustment or peer relations among the offspring of nonheterosexual parents.

The results of a recent study [by Jennifer L. Wainwright and Charlotte J. Patterson in "Peer Relationships Among Adolescents with Female Same-Sex Parents"] of peer relations among adolescents living with female same-sex couples are particularly important in addressing this question. These authors studied a nationally representative sample of adolescents in the United States and compared peer relations among those who lived with same-sex versus different-sex parenting couples. They studied peer reports as well as adolescents' own self-reports about friendships, activities with friends, and popularity among classmates. They also studied measures of density and centrality in peer networks. Across these and other measures of adolescent peer relations, there were no significant differences as a function of family type. In short, claims that youngsters' peer relations suffer when they live with same-sex couples are not supported by the findings of empirical research.

Children of Gay Parents Are Well Adjusted

More than 25 years of research on the offspring of nonheterosexual parents has yielded results of remarkable clarity. Regardless of whether researchers have studied the offspring of divorced lesbian and gay parents or those born to lesbian or gay parents, their findings have been similar. Regardless of whether researchers have studied children or adolescents, they have reported similar results. Regardless of whether investigators have examined sexual identity, self-esteem, adjustment, or qualities of social relationships, the results have been remarkably consistent. In study after study, the offspring of lesbian and gay parents have been found to be at least as well adjusted overall as those of other parents.

Despite the sometimes adverse legal climates in which many families live, results of research on children of lesbian and gay parents suggest that they develop in positive ways. Thus, the research findings provide no justification for limitations on child custody or visitation by lesbian or gay parents in divorce proceedings.

> "Children raised by two men or two
> women are missing a role model. It's
> important for a child to have a mom
> and dad in order to be secure in gender
> roles."

Gay Parents Should Not Be Granted Child Custody

John W. Kennedy

John W. Kennedy is news editor of Pentecostal Evangel *and served as news editor of* Christianity Today *for seven years.*

In the following viewpoint, Kennedy contends that there has been a significant increase in the number of lesbian and gay people attempting to form families through adoption, custody, and reproductive measures. Gays and lesbians have been active in attempting to secure the same parental rights as heterosexuals, asserts Kennedy. To support their claims, homosexuals often cite biased research; yet reliable research indicates that children fare better when they are raised in traditional families, Kennedy argues.

John W. Kennedy, "Gay Parenting on Trial," *Christianity Today*, July 8, 2002. Copyright © 2002 Christianity Today. Reproduced by permission of the author.

As you read, consider the following questions:

1. The author cites "self-presentation bias" to support his position that many studies on homosexual parenting are flawed. What causes this bias, according to the author?

2. What reasons does the author give for rejecting the study by the American Academy of Pediatrics supporting gay parenting?

3. Researchers Robert Lerner and Althea Nagai found mistakes in forty-nine studies on gay parenting. According to the author, what was one of their biggest concerns with the research?

Gays and lesbians are stepping up their national battle against restrictive state regulations, conservative Christians, and others to gain the same parenting rights as heterosexuals.

"There is no doubt that homosexuals love their children," says Suzanne Cook, a Christian who was raised in part by her divorced father living with his gay lover. "But it takes more than love to raise children in an appropriate and healthy way. We shouldn't be experimenting on another generation." ...

An Insider Relates Her Negative Experience

Cook, a resident of Fort Worth, Texas, has an insider's perspective on homosexual parenting. Cook told *Christianity Today* that when she was seven years old her father left the family to pursue a homosexual relationship. Three years later, her parents divorced but shared custody. Cook and her younger brother spent every other weekend at the apartment of her father's partner. "They did not refrain from having sex when we were there," Cook says. "They didn't come out of the bedroom until noon."

Cook says her father's partner molested her brother for the next several years. "I had to deal with keeping my brother

Children Raised by Homosexuals Are at Risk

Data on the long-term outcomes of children placed in homosexual households is sparse and gives reason for concern. This research has revealed that children reared in homosexual households are more likely to experience sexual confusion, engage in risky sexual experimentation, and later adopt a homosexual identity. This is concerning since adolescents and young adults who adopt the homosexual lifestyle are at increased risk for mental health problems.

American College of Pediatricians, "Homosexual Parenting: Is It Time for Change?" March 26, 2009. www.acpeds.org.

safe," Cook says. "I had to put on the role of a parent as a little kid. I felt the whole world on my shoulders." (Cook's father declined comment to *Christianity Today*.)

Confused about her sexuality as a young teenager, Cook supposed the only way to have a relationship with a man was to offer sex. Even her mother encouraged her to have sexual relations outside marriage so that she would not mistakenly wed a homosexual.

Cook's life included adultery, group sex, and an abortion. In time, her brother led Cook, now 44 and married for 16 years, to Christian faith.

Cook strongly supports a ban on gay adoptions. She says that children with homosexual parents avoid criticizing parental sexual behavior when responding to questions in research projects. (Experts say "self-presentation bias," in which those surveyed give an "overly positive picture of their family life," causes significant flaws in research.)

Civil Rights Shouldn't Trump Children's Rights

University of Southern California researchers Judith Stacey and Timothy J. Biblarz published an article titled "(How) Does the Sexual Orientation of Parents Matter?" last year [2001] in *American Sociological Review*. Stacey and Biblarz examined 21 gay-parenting studies. They concluded that there is "no notable difference between children reared by heterosexual parents and those reared by lesbian and gay parents."

Stacey, 59, told *Christianity Today* that society should consider the desires of adults as well as the welfare of children regarding gay parenting. "It's both a civil rights issue and a children's rights issue," she says.

The pro-gay Lambda Legal Defense [and Education] Fund, in a 1997 document, notes that "the last decade has seen a sharp rise among gay people planning and forming families through adoption, foster care, donor insemination, and other reproductive technologies. Some have described the current period as a lesbian and gay 'baby boom.'"

But homosexuals should not be permitted to adopt or provide foster care, because it's not in the best interest of children, said Alan Chambers, head of Exodus [International], a Christian ministry that assists individuals in overcoming homosexuality.

Some gay advocates are more interested in expanding their own civil rights than in providing stable homes for children, Chambers told *Christianity Today* in an interview. Courts have held there is no right to adopt.

An increasing number of individuals who contact Exodus have had homosexual parents, he said. "They were raised in gay-parent households, and it was detrimental to them, especially as they grew older."

Chambers says children raised by two men or two women are missing a role model. "It's important for a child to have a mom and dad in order to be secure in gender roles," Chambers says. "Even though a divorce situation isn't ideal, there are still significant male and female relationships patterned."

Researcher Error Is Alleged

In forming public policy and applying existing law, judges and state officials often look to doctors and social scientists to assess how homosexual parents influence young children and what is in the best interest of a minor child who is orphaned or whose parents have divorced.

In turn, gay advocates urge politicians, doctors, and researchers to believe that homosexuals can be good parents and should be allowed to adopt or retain child custody after a divorce. Rosie O'Donnell, media celebrity and parent to three adopted children, declared on national television, "I am the gay parent."

Janet Reno, a [one-time] Democratic candidate for governor of Florida, has pledged her support for overturning her state's ban on gay adoptions.

Homosexual activists have commended the American Academy of Pediatrics (AAP) for a February [2001] statement that "a growing body of scientific literature demonstrates that children who grow up with one or two gay or lesbian parents fare as well in emotional, cognitive, social, and sexual functioning as do children whose parents are heterosexual." The academy urged its 55,000 members to support "second-parent" adoptions, in which a homosexual adopts a partner's children.

Conservative rejection of the AAP announcement was swift. British sociologist Patricia Morgan, author of *Children As Trophies?* told *Christianity Today*, "There's a tremendous bias in both the publishing and acceptance" of results that support homosexual parenting.

Morgan, who has written extensively on family development, says that four dozen studies cited by the AAP are in error because researchers failed to use control groups, used self-selected volunteers, and relied on nonrandom samples.

Morgan, senior research fellow at London's Institute for the Study of Civil Society, says research supportive of gay parenting shows a tendency toward "extravagant claims" from sympathetic researchers. "Any critical evaluation or examination of the work . . . is apt to invoke furious reflex accusations about homophobia."

Researchers Robert Lerner and Althea Nagai, coauthors of *No Basis: What the Studies Don't Tell Us About Same-Sex Parenting*, support Morgan's findings. Lerner and Nagai evaluated 49 studies on gay parenting, finding significant mistakes in all of them.

They particularly criticized "convenience sampling," in which investigators select whoever is available, and "snowball sampling," in which homosexual activists help researchers find volunteers willing to answer questions.

"These studies prove nothing," Lerner and Nagai wrote. They say reliance on this suspect research has strongly influenced policy makers toward a positive view of gay parenting.

Morgan believes the most reliable research clearly shows that "children reared in a home with a married mother and father do far better than children in other circumstances."

She criticizes the current tendency to tout homosexual parenting despite the evidence against it. "We can't compromise where there are moral standards or empirical standards," Morgan says. "Both have been compromised at the moment."

> "Grandparents, traditionally regarded as second-level parents and often charged with the care of grandchildren, deserve notice and preference in custody proceedings concerning their grandchildren, if they have assumed a parent-like role in the child's life."

Sometimes Grandparents Should Be Awarded Custody

Michelle Ognibene

Michelle Ognibene is a senior associate in the regulatory and government affairs department at the law firm WilmerHale.

The custody statutes of many states fail to protect the interests of grandparents, sometimes to the extent of giving foster care preference over custody by grandparents, contends Ognibene in the following viewpoint. In cases where loving grandparents have established strong emotional bonds with a child, they deserve preference in custody hearings when parents are unable to care for the children, the author argues.

Michelle Ognibene, "A Constitutional Analysis of Grandparents' Custody Rights," *University of Chicago Law Review*, vol. 72, Fall 2005, pp. 1474–77, 1480, 1495–99. Reproduced by permission of The University of Chicago Law Review conveyed through Copyright Clearance Center, Inc.

As you read, consider the following questions:

1. What can result when a state fails to require notice to grandparents of the custody arrangements for a child?

2. The author argues that grandparents should receive consideration under the due process clause. What rights to the child would be conveyed under this clause?

3. While due process wouldn't guarantee that grandparents be granted custody, it would afford them an important protection. What is this protection?

Many state statutes contain a preference for grants of custody to those who would likely have the closest emotional ties to the child. This policy preference, however, seldom gives grandparents the same procedural guarantees as those that parents enjoy in custody proceedings. Generally, state law does not require petitioners for adoption to notify grandparents of adoption proceedings, nor does it require grandparents' consent. Courts may even deny grandparents the right to intervene in parental rights termination proceedings, potentially allowing the state to take custody of the child without affording the grandparents an opportunity to express their preferences or offer an alternative home for the child. This result appears particularly harsh in light of the fact that adoption can mean the end of the grandparents' relationship with the child. Several courts, condemning these results, have required notice to grandparents of adoption hearings because of their interest in the proceedings.

Once the child has been removed from his family, his grandparents' ability to petition for his adoption can be significantly inhibited by a lack of notice of custody proceedings, competing adoption petitions, or any sort of deference to the parent-like roles and obligations that grandparents often assume. Despite evidence of a policy preference in many states for kinship care over foster care, grandparents still may be at a disadvantage in adoption competitions with foster parents. By explicitly preferring foster parents and strangers to the family, as at least one state does, and by failing to require notice or a hearing for grandparents, adoption and custody statutes may unduly interfere with any rights grandparents may have to direct the upbringing of their grandchildren. . . .

The Rights of Grandparents Should Be Protected

The interests of grandparents in their relationships with their grandchildren bear many similarities to those of parents. Grandparents and parents generally share similar feelings of love and responsibility for the child, and grandparents often assist parents in caring for the child. These similarities demonstrate that the interests of grandparents deserve protection under the due process clause[1] as both important personal relationships and as an extension of parental autonomy rights. . . .

Loving Grandparents Should Get Preference over Foster Care

Grandparents often assume traditional parental roles with the parents' explicit or implicit consent. For example, grandparents frequently act as babysitters, or grandparents may take grandchildren into their homes when parents are not able to provide adequate care. In cases where grandparents have formed these relationships with their grandchildren, they deserve protection from state interference, as required by the due process clause. . . .

If a grandparent's interest in adoption falls under the protection of the due process clause, that protection warrants a requirement to notify grandparents whenever adoption petitions or custody orders contrary to their interests are filed.

---

1. Under the due process clause of the Fourteenth Amendment, citizens who are a party to legal hearings are guaranteed that their rights shall be upheld and that they will have a voice in any legal proceedings.

Custodial Grandparents Receive Little Support

The 2000 census revealed that one in twelve children under age 18 lives in a home headed by a grandparent. . . . [The] majority of children living with grandparent(s) are not in custody of the child welfare system. The grandparent(s) provide a safety net to children inside and outside the social welfare system. . . . Although this informal, private or voluntary arrangement has many advantages for the child, there are fewer resources available to the kin caregiver.

Sally Raphel,
"Kinship Care and the Situation for Grandparents,"
Journal of Child and Adolescent Psychiatric Nursing,
May 2008.

This notice requirement could be limited to situations where the child is no longer in the parents' care and where the grandparents appear to have established a substantial relationship with the child. Courts could easily ascertain the existence of such a relationship by a brief interview with the child, or by an inquiry into the circumstances of the parental rights termination. . . .

More significantly, due process would also require that grandparents' adoption petitions receive preferential consideration where grandparents can demonstrate the necessary relationship criteria. First, the preference would ensure that grandparents have standing to object to foster care orders that are contrary to their interests. Second, the preference could require the court to weigh more heavily grandparents' interests in caring for the child over the alternative of putting the child into foster care.

Such a pre-foster care preference would avert many conflicts between grandparents and foster parents, while minimizing disruption in the child's life. This preference would also protect grandparents' significant liberty interest in the companionship of their grandchildren and the power to direct their upbringing in the absence of parents. The preference could also enhance grandparents' abilities to petition for visitation if their grandchildren are placed in foster care. Currently, grandparents' interests are at their most vulnerable once the child is placed with strangers to the family. If, however, courts recognize a constitutionally protected liberty interest in grandparent-grandchild relationships, grandparents will be guaranteed standing and their petitions will bear more weight in custody and visitation disputes.

Preference in custody proceedings would not guarantee that grandparents will prevail in every case in which they assert an interest. Rather, the best interests of the child analysis would continue to serve as a restriction on grandparents' rights, just as the best interests of the child can now override parents' rights in cases of neglect or abuse. Instead, the proposed adoption preference for grandparents would merely establish a rebuttable presumption of their fitness as adoptive parents and custodians.

This proposed preference may seem like a small step for grandparents' rights, for it says nothing about how a court must weigh their interests after the child has entered into foster care for an extended period of time. The preference, however, can avert substantial dislocation for the child by ensuring that grandparents have access to the courts before the child enters foster care. . . .

Although due process protection of grandparents' adoption rights provides no guarantees that grandparents' custody petitions will always be successful, the protection would ensure that grandparents—whom many cases, statutes, and traditions regard as uniquely important in a child's life—are not separated from their grandchildren by state action without good reason and adequate deliberation. The protection applies in a narrow set of circumstances, preventing the severance of existing relationships and family units rather than automatically deferring to grandparents simply because of their position in the family tree.

The Supreme Court has long emphasized the essential importance and constitutional protection of the right to direct the upbringing of children. These cases have generally defined this right in terms of the parent-child relationship; however, there are significant indications that it can apply equally to grandparents when they assume a similar role in inculcating values and providing for the child's physical and emotional needs. The autonomy rights of parents strictly circumscribe the scope of any right grandparents possess. In situations where the parents are unavailable or unfit, however, and grandparents have previously enjoyed a role in the child's life, state action should not interfere with that relationship unless its continuance is contrary to the child's best interests.

Grandparents, traditionally regarded as second-level parents and often charged with the care of grandchildren, deserve notice and preference in custody proceedings concerning their grandchildren, if they have assumed a parent-like role in the child's life. Statutes that fail to prefer kinship or grandparent care over foster care, or that fail to require foster parents to notify grandparents of an intention to adopt, unconstitutionally curtail this right. Unless the overarching requirements of the best interests of the child dictate otherwise, these grandparents' interests should enjoy preference in an evaluation of competing petitions for adoption by strangers to the family.

The recognition of a fundamental liberty interest in the custody and care of grandchildren does not preclude the success of all other potentially qualified candidates in adoption proceedings. It merely ensures that states will give grandparents with substantial relationships with their grandchildren a sufficient opportunity to voice their desire to adopt and to have their important familial ties and family-specific benefits adequately considered.

> *"Despite limitations, our findings suggest that custodial grandchildren are at greater risk of mental health problems than children in general."*

Children Raised by Grandparents Are at Risk for Emotional Problems

Gregory C. Smith and Patrick A. Palmieri

Gregory C. Smith is affiliated with the College of Education, Health, and Human Services of Kent State University. Patrick A. Palmieri is with the Summa-Kent State Center for the Treatment and Study of Traumatic Stress and with the Department of Psychology of Kent State University.

Smith and Palmieri conducted a study funded by the National Institute of Mental Health on custodial grandmothers. Data from the 733 custodial grandparents participating in this study were compared to data from 9,878 caregivers from the general population surveyed in 2001 in the National Health Interview Survey. The authors concluded that children raised by custodial grandmothers fared worse than the control group across

Gregory C. Smith and Patrick A. Palmieri, "Risk of Psychological Difficulties Among Children Raised by Custodial Grandparents," *Psychiatric Services*, vol. 58, October 2007, pp. 1303–04, 1307, 1309. Reprinted with permission from Psychiatric Services, (Copyright 2007). American Psychiatric Association.

all categories studied. In the following viewpoint, the authors contend that custodial grandchildren are more likely to have behavioral and emotional problems than children in the general population.

As you read, consider the following questions:

1. What two reasons do the authors cite to back their contention that custodial grandchildren are at greater risk of emotional and behavioral problems than children in general?

2. What statistics do the authors cite from a study by Harinder S. Ghuman and colleagues to support their position?

3. What additional research is needed on custodial grandchildren, according to the authors?

Although increasing numbers of grandparents are becoming surrogate parents to grandchildren, little is known about how custodial grandchildren fare in these families. Yet there are two major reasons why custodial grandchildren may encounter greater risk of behavioral and emotional difficulties than children in general. One reason is that custodial grandchildren typically receive care from grandparents because of such predicaments among their parents as substance abuse, child abuse and neglect, teenage pregnancy, death, illness, divorce, incarceration, and HIV-AIDS. Such predicaments bear numerous risks of psychopathology among custodial grandchildren, including exposure to prenatal toxins, early childhood trauma, insufficient interaction with parents, family conflict, uncertainty about the future, and societal stigma.

Another reason why custodial grandchildren may experience higher risk of emotional and behavioral difficulties concerns the numerous challenges that grandparents face as caregivers. For many this role is developmentally off time, un-

planned, ambiguous, and undertaken with considerable am-
bivalence. Additional challenges to raising custodial grandchildren include inadequate support, social stigma, isolation,
disrupted leisure and retirement plans, age-related adversities,
anger toward grandchildren's parents, and financial strain.
Thus, custodial grandparents typically show elevated rates of
anxiety, irritability, anger, and guilt. Such heightened psychological strain among parental figures is troubling because
abundant research shows that psychological distress is associated with increased dysfunctional parenting, which, in turn,
negatively affects children's psychological well-being. Recently,
it was found that psychological distress among custodial
grandmothers results in lower-quality parenting, which ultimately leads to higher maladjustment of custodial grandchildren.

There Are Few Studies on
Custodial Grandchildren

Despite these speculations that custodial grandchildren may
experience greater mental health difficulties than children in
general, scant research has examined the well-being of custodial grandchildren in comparison with other children. A hand-
ful of studies, however, provide preliminary evidence that custodial grandchildren do face higher risk. For instance,
[Harinder S.] Ghuman and colleagues found [in "Demo-
graphic and Clinical Characteristics of Emotionally Disturbed
Children Being Raised by Grandparents"] that 22% of 233
youths attending an inner-city community mental health center for treatment of psychological difficulties were cared for by
grandparents. Although this rate was disproportionately higher
than the 6% of all children living in a grandparent's household, generalizability of these findings is unknown because the
sample was restricted to custodial grandchildren from a single
clinic. . . .

The Study Shows Children at Risk

Our study is the first to examine risk of emotional and behavioral difficulties among custodial grandchildren from a large, national data set and uses a well-established measure of psychological adjustment. We asked a national sample of 366 black and 367 white custodial grandmothers to complete the Strengths and Difficulties Questionnaire (SDQ) in regard to a target grandchild. The SDQ is a psychometrically sound measure of the psychological adjustment of children. . . .

Our findings provide new evidence that custodial grandchildren of both genders are at greater risk of psychological difficulties than children in the general population. Statistically significant mean differences with correspondingly large effect sizes were observed between the custodial grandchildren and NHIS [National Health Interview Survey] samples on each domain measured by the SDQ. . . .

Despite limitations, our findings suggest that custodial grandchildren are at greater risk of mental health problems than children in general. Given the dearth of research on the well-being of custodial grandchildren, we hope that this study will draw further attention to the needs of custodial grandchildren and their caregivers. Additional research is needed to determine the rates of specific diagnosable disorders experienced by custodial grandchildren, the underlying reasons for these disorders, and whether they vary by key sociodemographic and cultural influences.

"Over the last 25 years, as the divorce
rate has climbed, the courts and family
therapists have seen a rise in the number of cases in which children have become strongly allied with one parent
and alienated from the other parent."

Parental Alienation Syndrome Should Be Considered in Custody Cases

Elizabeth M. Ellis

Elizabeth M. Ellis is a psychologist in Duluth, Georgia. She is the author of Divorce Wars: Interventions with Families in Conflict.

In the following viewpoint, Ellis describes parental alienation syndrome (PAS), a condition identified by child psychologist Richard A. Gardner in the 1980s. In cases of PAS, a child will ally strongly with one parent and reject the other, explains Ellis. The parents of a child with PAS typically have gone through a bitter divorce, and the alienating parent, usually the mother, will demonize her former husband to the child. According to Ellis, clini-

Elizabeth M. Ellis, "Help for the Alienated Parent," *The American Journal of Family Therapy*, vol. 33, 2005. Copyright © 2005 Taylor & Francis Group, LLC. Reproduced by permission of Taylor & Francis, Ltd., http://www.informaworld.com.

cians need to be mindful of PAS when dealing with children impacted by parental conflict.

As you read, consider the following questions:

1. What causes did Gardner see for PAS?

2. In Johnston's study of children in the nine to thirteen age group, she found a portion of the children who allied strongly with one parent while rejecting the other. What reasons did she see for this behavior?

3. How do Johnston and Campbell describe the dynamics of how PAS develops?

Over the last 25 years, as the divorce rate has climbed, the courts and family therapists have seen a rise in the number of cases in which children have become strongly allied with one parent and alienated from the other parent. [Judith] Wallerstein and [Joan] Kelly, studying 131 children from divorcing families in California in the 1970s, found a small portion of them—about 25%—to be strongly allied with their mothers after a very conflicted divorce. They joined in with their mothers in waging a campaign of denigration and rejection of their fathers. Wallerstein and Kelly referred to these children as "refusers" and noted that the children were mostly older—between the ages of 9 and 12. Mother-son dyads [pairs] were the most common pair. Many of these children appeared to be angry at the father for his contribution to the divorce. Some had never had a strong relationship with the father and were uncomfortable with fathers, who made little effort to nurture, understand, or accommodate them. Richard [A.] Gardner [in the 1980s] coined the term parental alienation syndrome (PAS) to describe this pattern and the term has become part of our lexicon in describing these children. In Gardner's cases, 90% of the children were in mother custody homes, were allied with the mother, and were alienated from their fathers. Gardner saw the problem as stemming in large part by active efforts on the part of the mother to sever the child's relationship with the father. He attributed this to changes in divorce law that threatened the primary and custodial control of mothers, especially stay-at-home mothers.

Parental Alienation Syndrome Is Controversial

While PAS has been the lightning rod for controversy and has engendered much debate in the literature and on Web sites, little actual data is available. [John] Dunne and [Marsha] Hedrick (1994) studied 16 families which met Gardner's criteria for PAS. Of the 26 children in these families, 21 were "involved in the alienation dynamic" with a parent. Mother-daughter dyads were most common. [Robert J.] Racusin, [Stuart A.] Copans, and [Peter] Mills (1994) studied 12 children who were "refusers," and found girls and boys to be equally prevalent. Most were the oldest child in the family and were likely to be oldest daughters. They also found the parents to have high levels of emotional problems. [Janet R.] Johnston (1993) reported on 175 children seen in highly conflicted divorces, some of which formed strong "alignments" with one parent. She found alignments to be most common in the 9 to 12 age group.

Johnston and her group of researchers in California have steadfastly avoided the PAS terminology—no doubt to avoid the controversy associated with it—and have consistently referred to these cases as "children in alignments." Their original study [published in 1988] consisted of 100 children of 80 divorcing parents who were in the process of divorcing when they were referred by the courts for counseling and mediation. Their second sample [published in 1992] consisted of 75 children who were referred by the family courts whose divorced parents had been involved in domestic violence or protracted post-divorce disputes for several years. Johnston described the process of how children form alliances. She found that a por-

Actor Alec Baldwin Was a Victim of Parental Alienation Syndrome

Whether PAS [parental alienation syndrome] rises to the level of a psychological syndrome is for scientists and the courts to decide. In the meantime, the problem of parental alienation must be addressed. This is more than a legal or psychological issue. At its core, parental alienation is a form of child abuse, for the child is the ultimate victim. The alienating parent chooses to cut the child off from one of the most important relationships in that child's life. As a result, the child will be far more susceptible to a wide range of problems than those who have a good relationship with both parents. Studies show that children who grow up in a single-parent home are far more likely to abuse drugs and alcohol, to engage in unsafe sexual behavior, to get in trouble with legal authorities, and to perform poorly in school. Children who grow up under the care of an alienating parent have significantly greater problems in forming attachments in their adult lives, as they have been taught to push down and, therefore, mistrust their own innate feelings toward others. While children of divorce are also more susceptible to these social problems, the effects are lessened when both parents take an active role in the child's life. The alienating parent ignores this fact and risks that the child will potentially have a more difficult and less fulfilling life. Meanwhile, the child is powerless to do anything about it.

Whatever the reasons that an alienating parent gives for their actions, common sense dictates that one need not see a pattern of behavior listed in a psychiatric manual to understand that this problem is real and destroying the lives of parents and children everywhere.

Alec Baldwin, A Promise to Ourselves: A Journey Through Fatherhood and Divorce. New York: St. Martin's Press, 2008.

tion of the children in the 9 to 13 age group, having been exposed to the inter-parental conflict for several years, began to "make strong alliances, these being overtly hostile, unshakable stances in which the child may stridently reject and refuse to see or visit one parent." She reasoned that the children began to do so because of a convergence of several factors. The children in this age group were old enough to be aware of and to understand some of the complex dynamics of their parents' conflict, they had a tendency to adopt a polarized moral view of the situation, and they often were under some subtle, or not so subtle, pressure from family members to "take a stand." Comparing their sample with the Wallerstein and Kelly sample, they found that these cases also occurred more frequently where the litigation was "chronic" and the hostility was "unremitting." Thus, their group of children ages 9 to 12 had been exposed to intense levels of conflict for several years. Twenty-five percent to 40% of them had formed an alignment with one parent and were consistently denigrating and rejecting the other parent. In extreme cases the child's distortion of reality and perceptions of the alienated parent as particularly evil and horrible took on a bizarre quality. They referred to these strong alignments as "closely related to PAS" as defined by Gardner.

Parental Alienation Is Seen as a Solution by the Child

Johnston and [Linda E.] Campbell (1988) further elaborated what they saw to be the dynamics of how PAS develops. With samples of children of various ages, they were able to chart the responses of children to conflicted visitations and inter-parental hostility and note how the response patterns change with development. Six- to eight-year-olds were characterized by intense emotional distress over trying to be loyal to both parents. Some of this distress dropped off as they got older and "were old enough to take a stand." Thus, forming an alliance with one parent and rejecting another was seen as a way to reduce anxiety and confusion. This is a key insight into working with these children in that the PAS, while an irresolvable conundrum for the courts and family therapists, is not the *problem* for the child but rather the *solution* to the problem. Thus it is not ego dystonic, and the child is not eager or typically willing to give it up.

Johnston and Campbell also found that these children had typically been compliant children who had overly close, enmeshed, even dependent relationships with their mothers. The mothers appeared to not have recovered emotionally from the divorce but were still hurt, angry, and depressed. The parents' separation, in their sample of highly conflicted divorces, was particularly traumatic and had involved physical abuse, abandonment, or betrayal. The mothers had experienced unusual degrees of humiliation, demoralization, fear, and/or helplessness. In many of these cases, the injured parent communicates to the children, subtle or overtly, that the children's loyalty to her is "all I have."

In the post-divorce custodial household, the alienated parent began to be seen in increasingly negative terms as the "all bad" parent. The injured parent projected all blame for the divorce on the other parent in an attempt to salvage their own dignity and self-esteem. The children in these households increasingly began to mirror the alienating parent's emotions, actions, and statements. Every angry, retaliatory action taken by the alienated parent, in his attempt to gain access to the children, was used as further evidence that he was cruel, unsympathetic, and villainous, and that the mother-child unit was being victimized. As the children grew increasingly allied with the injured parent, the injured parent grew stronger and the children were seen as less distressed. So, for the alienating parent as well, the PAS problem was not the *problem* but the *solution* to the problem.

The alignment was often fueled by people in the community allying with the alienating parent, to form strong "coalitions" allied against the alienated parent. These were naturally the alienating parent's relatives and attorney, which is to be expected. However, caseworkers, teachers, even coaches, and the child's therapist were often drawn into the coalition by submitting affidavits to the court, colluding to block contact between the child and alienated parent, suppressing information about the child's whereabouts and the child's day-to-day activities.

In terms of its developmental course, they found that children who were very young when their parents divorced were more likely to become aligned than those whose parents divorced later. These children had no positive memories of the intact family, had no history of a positive bond with the alienated parent, and thus had never formed such a bond. They also found these children, due to their enmeshment and alignment, had not developed good boundaries and a coherent sense of self. These alliances were extremely resistant to intervention and often persisted through adolescence. They had no data on the eventual outcome of these cases. As of this writing [2005], there exists no data on the long-range outcome for these children as they move into young adulthood.

| "The most notorious junk science theory used in custody cases is parental alienation syndrome (PAS)."

Parental Alienation Syndrome Should Not Be Considered in Custody Cases

Trish Wilson

Trish Wilson is an editor for Expository Magazine.

Parental alienation syndrome (PAS), a theory developed by psychologist Richard A. Gardner to explain false cases of child abuse in his practice, has been used to unfairly take children from their mothers and place them with their fathers, according to Wilson in the following viewpoint. PAS is not recognized as a legitimate condition by responsible members of the psychological profession, Wilson contends. Wilson further argues that despite the fact that PAS has not been proven, it is increasingly being used by lawyers to justify custody for fathers.

As you read, consider the following questions:

1. In most of the cases of PAS that Gardner identified, what remedy did he recommend?

Trish Wilson, "Discredited Junk Science Justifies Custody for Fathers," *off our backs*, January–February 2004, pp. 46–48. Copyright © 2004 off our backs, inc. Reproduced by permission.

2. What are two areas of concern with PAS being used in court to determine custody, according to Carol Bruch?

3. Douglas Darnall is a psychologist who has developed a similar theory of parental alienation. What reasons does the author give for discrediting his methods?

An unfounded psychological theory that has been used to unfairly wrest child custody from mothers threatens to influence more custody cases, even after these theories were discredited.

In some of the worst cases many mothers have been forced to file for bankruptcy as a result of the exorbitant fees paid to court-ordered psychological evaluators, and their contact with the children is severely curtailed.

Parental Alienation Syndrome Is Junk Science

The most notorious junk science theory used in custody cases is parental alienation syndrome (PAS). Child psychologist Richard [A.] Gardner coined PAS in 1985 to describe what he believed to be a high number of false allegations of child sexual abuse in his personal caseload. According to Gardner's theory, "the child viciously vilifies one of the parents and idealizes the other" and in 80 to 90 percent of the cases the father is the vilified one.

In the vast majority of PAS cases in his caseload, Gardner recommended the removal of the children from the mother's home and placement with the father, and following this transfer recommended a "period of decompression and debriefing in which the mother has no opportunity at all for input to the children . . . to give the children the opportunity to reestablish the relationship with the alienated father, without significant contamination of the process by the brainwashing mother."

Gardner's theory is based, in part, on findings of Judith Wallerstein and Joan Kelly that upon divorce children some-

Parental Alienation Syndrome Is Often Misused

Divorcing parents have long bashed each other in hopes of winning points with kids. But today, the strategy of blame encompasses a psychological concept of parental alienation that is increasingly used—and misused—in the courts.

On the one hand, with so many contentious divorces, [some] parents ... have been tragically alienated from the children they love. On the other hand, parental alienation has been seized as a strategic tool in custody fights, its effects exploited in the courtroom, often to the detriment of loving parents protecting children from true neglect or abuse. With the impact of alienation so devastating—and false accusations so prevalent—it may take a judge with the wisdom of Solomon to differentiate between the two faces of alienation: a truly toxic parent and his or her victimized children versus manipulation of the legal system to claim damage where none exists.

Mark Teich, "A Divided House: Hate Thy Father,"
Psychology Today, *May/June 2007.*

times align with one parent and reject the other—without taking into account that in all but the cases involving the most violent families, those children resolved their behavior as they matured. Reputable psychological and medical professionals do not recognize PAS as a valid syndrome, nor does the American Psychological Association recognize it as a mental disorder, and it has not been peer reviewed in psychological journals. Gardner's books are self-published, and they are not held at most university and research libraries. Gardner has provided no research findings to substantiate his claims about his syndrome. It is merely his opinion based upon his personal observations of cases in his private practice.

His professional peers have expressed their disdain for PAS. Dr. Paul J. Fink, a past president of the American Psychiatric Association, ... has stated, "PAS as a scientific theory has been excoriated by legitimate researchers across the nation. Judged solely on his merits, Dr. Gardner should be a rather pathetic footnote or an example of poor scientific standards."

PAS Is Often Rejected in the Courts

When Gardner's testimony on the validity of PAS itself has been challenged in court it has usually been rejected. Professor Emerita and Research Professor of Law at University of California, Davis, Carol Bruch says these cases "reveal two areas of concern. First, courts are consistent in refusing to permit Gardner to testify on the truth or falsity of witnesses, noting that this question is reserved to the trier of fact. Second, most US courts considering the question agree that PAS has not been generally accepted by professionals and does not meet the applicable test for scientific reliability."

Despite the widespread condemnation of PAS, it continues to appear in courtrooms, presumably because attorneys can use it to make a scientific-sounding argument to give custody to the father.

In recent years, PAS has been greatly expanded to include cases of all sorts in which a child refuses to visit the noncustodial parent, regardless of whether or not sexual abuse allegations have been made. The definition of "alienation" has broadened to mean "difficulties stemming from the child's disproportionate, persistent, and unreasonable negative feelings and beliefs towards a parent."

Another Alienation Proponent Is Not Respected by Peers

Psychologist Douglas Darnall is an "alienation" proponent who works in private practice and serves as the court psychologist for Trumbull County Family Court in Warren, Ohio. He describes "parental alienation," which he differentiates from PAS, as "any constellation of behaviors, whether conscious or unconscious, that could evoke a disturbance in the relationship between a child and the other parent." These expanded and vague definitions leave the door open for professional abuses and malicious allegations to be made against mothers.

Like Gardner, Darnall has not won recognition by his peers. In fact, he faced allegations by the Ohio State Board of Psychology that in his private practice he engaged in professional misconduct, including negligence, impaired objectivity and dual relationships, lack of regard for the welfare of the client, and incompetence. Like PAS, Darnall's alienation theory continues to find its way into the courts.

Conflict of Interest Is Alleged in Some Cases

In another case of junk science being used as a weapon against parents and children, the New York Post reported on charges placed against a group of highly paid mental health experts and child guardians who were recruited by the company Soft Split LCC. They promoted their services on a website that offered "tips on how to negotiate divorce and custody fights." Some experts also participated in online chat rooms accessed through the site. Big-name clientele included former [New York City] Mayor Rudy Giuliani, Revlon CEO Ron Perelman and publishing queen Judith Regan.

A group of mothers and fathers who questioned the ethics of this practice filed suit, saying "that business link was never revealed in court when some of the experts were assigned by judges to at least eight known cases." One unnamed parent cited in the article "was shocked to discover that her ex-husband's lawyer was part of Soft Split—along with all four experts assigned by the court to her case. The woman's lawyer demanded a conflict-of-interest hearing in February, during which three Soft Split experts admitted that they had hoped to make money from their affiliation with the Web company."

The group of parents formed their own support group, the Family Justice Project. They seek to reform the New York child custody proceedings so that children's best interests are protected.

Periodical and Internet Sources Bibliography

The following articles have been selected to supplement the diverse views presented in this chapter.

Lorraine Ali	"Mrs. Kramer vs. Mrs. Kramer," *Newsweek*, December 6, 2008. www.newsweek.com.
Sandra Baum and Jan Burns	"Mothers with Learning Disabilities: Experiences and Meanings of Losing Custody of Their Children," *Learning Disability Review*, vol. 12, no. 3, July 2007.
Elizabeth M. Ellis	"Should a Psychotherapist Be Compelled to Release an Adolescent's Treatment Records to a Parent in a Contested Custody Case?" *Professional Psychology: Research & Practice*, vol. 40, no. 6, December 2009.
Linda D. Elrod and Milfred D. Dale	"Paradigm Shifts and Pendulum Swings in Child Custody: The Interests of Children in the Balance," *Family Law Quarterly*, vol. 42, no. 3, Fall 2008.
Robert E. Emery, Randy K. Otto, and William O'Donohue	"Custody Disputed," *Scientific American Mind*, October 2005.
Gregory A. Hession	"Former Lesbian Lover Awarded Custody of Non-Biological Children," *New American*, October 20, 2009.
Janice H. Laakso and Sheri Adams	"Noncustodial Fathers' Involvement with Their Children: A Right or a Privilege?" *Families in Society*, vol. 87, no. 1, January–March 2006.
Dahlia Lithwick	"Whose God Wins?" *Newsweek*, February 26, 2010. www.newsweek.com.
Leo Strupczewski	"Gay Parents Have Equal Standing in Custody Cases," *Legal Intelligencer*, January 25, 2010.

OPPOSING
VIEWPOINTS®
SERIES

CHAPTER 2

How Should Custody Be Determined for Adopted Children?

Chapter Preface

Triggering what would become a landmark adoption custody battle, a single woman from Iowa, Cara Clausen, became pregnant out of wedlock in 1990. Clausen had been dating Scott Seefeldt, after breaking up with her former boyfriend, Dan Schmidt, and she named Seefeldt as the father of her baby girl. Shortly after the birth, Clausen and Seefeldt surrendered their parental rights. A Michigan couple seeking a private adoption, Jan and Roberta DeBoer, learned of the availability of the infant and were able to take her home with them six days after her birth, instituting private adoption procedures that would have made them full legal custodians within six months. They named the baby Jessica.

Clausen quickly regretted her decision to give up the baby for adoption and informed Schmidt that he was the biological father of the little girl. Clausen and Schmidt married, and he petitioned to regain their baby, whom they called Anna, stating he had never given up his paternal rights. The case was tried in several courts in both Iowa and Michigan, and eventually Schmidt prevailed. The case was in the public eye for more than two years, and most news reports portrayed the well-educated DeBoers as being better able to provide for the child than the blue-collar Schmidts. In the years to follow, both couples divorced, with Dan Schmidt gaining custody of Anna from his ex-wife. Anna stated in 2003 that she had no memory of her time with the DeBoers and had enjoyed a happy childhood. The case was important in publicizing the risk of private adoptions. It also triggered a debate about whether the blood rights of parents are more important than providing a child a stable and secure environment.

Sara Wheeler and Melody Wheeler were lesbian partners who decided that they wanted a child. Following artificial insemination, Sara Wheeler gave birth to a son in January 2000, whom Melody Wheeler adopted in 2002 in a process termed second-parent adoption. The couple split two years later and commenced a bitter custody battle. Sara Wheeler petitioned to have the adoption overturned, claiming that homosexual adoption was not valid in the state of Georgia. In a divided opinion, the Supreme Court of Georgia declined to hear her case. While deciding whether to seek further legal action, the former partners shared visitation with the child. Legal experts lamented the lack of a clear opinion on a case that could have established a precedent for custody rights when same-sex relationships break up.

The history of adoption in the United States has evolved from the goal of addressing the needs of homeless children, which was the situation up until the middle of the twentieth century, to allowing infertile couples to build a family. Following the end of World War II, the standard adoption involved an unmarried Caucasian mother giving a newborn up for adoption to a Caucasian couple. For several decades, the supply of children to be adopted and the demand by couples wanting to adopt were approximately equal. The social upheaval of the 1960s and 1970s changed this picture. The legalization of abortion, widespread use of more effective birth control measures, and the increased social acceptance of unwed mothers keeping their babies led to a shortage of adoptable infants. In the 1970s, the number of newborn infants available for adoption decreased, and adoptions increased of harder-to-place children, including biracial children, children with handicaps or special needs, and siblings. By the 1980s, international adoption increased in popularity. Currently, approximately 15 percent of all American adoptions are of U.S.-born infants, 60 percent come from the child welfare system and are typically older children, and 25 percent are international adoptions. Each year, there are more than one hundred thousand children in foster care awaiting adoption.

Additionally, the profile of those seeking to adopt has changed. In a desire to have harder-to-place children adopted, social agencies have changed their restrictions, which used to require adoption into a two-parent family. Today, single men and women and couples in same-sex unions are able to adopt children, both domestically and internationally.

As society changes and the profiles of both the adoptive parents and the children to be adopted have changed, issues not contemplated by existing laws arise. The viewpoints in the chapter that follows debate how the best interests of the child can be upheld in determining the custody of adopted children.

> "[Dr. Stephen Erich's] two-decade study on gay parents and their children ... concludes that there is no empirical evidence that would suggest that growing up with gay parents would negatively impact their well-being."

Gay Adoption Should Be Permitted

Maria Carmela Sioco

Maria Carmela Sioco is an editorial intern at the Child Welfare League of America.

In the following viewpoint, Sioco examines adoption by homosexual individuals as made evident in a case in Florida, the only state in the country that specifically bans adoption to homosexual parents. A gay couple with two foster children appealed this ban and won in court, with a Miami-Dade circuit judge calling the ban unconstitutional and granting adoption rights to Martin Gill and his partner. The state attorney general's office filed an appeal, which as of May 2010 awaited a decision. During the testimony, numerous expert witnesses testified that

Maria Carmela Sioco, "What Makes a Family? A Closer Look at Gay Adoption," *Children's Voice*, vol. 18, no. 6, November–December 2009, pp. 18–23. Copyright Child Welfare League of America. All Rights Reserved. Reproduced by permission.

decades' worth of research conclusively proves that the parents' sexual orientation does not negatively impact a child, according to Sioco.

As you read, consider the following questions:

1. What are some of the organizations that testified against gay adoption during the Martin Gill trial?

2. What was the position of the Child Welfare League of America [CWLA] during the Martin Gill trial?

3. What were some of Dr. Stephen Erich's specific findings in support of gay adoption?

On October 14 [2009], the United States Supreme Court declined to review a challenge by the Liberty Counsel about the Florida Bar's amicus brief [a brief by a third party not involved in litigation supporting the position of one side] in support of Martin Gill, a gay man who sought to adopt his two foster children. Gill made history last year [2008] when Miami-Dade Circuit Judge Cindy Lederman struck down a 32-year law prohibiting gays and lesbians from adopting. The Liberty Counsel claimed that the Florida Bar was not authorized to use membership fees in supporting ideological causes not related to the legal profession. The Supreme Court voted 5-2, and denied review of Liberty Counsel's case, without comment.

Gill and his partner of nine years have been foster parents to James, 4, and John, 8, since 2004 through the Florida Department of Children and Families, a CWLA [Child Welfare League of America] member agency. But Gill isn't a typical prospective parent in the eyes of federal law—he is a gay man seeking to adopt in Florida, the only state in the country that has an outright ban on adopting to homosexual parents.

With the legal backing of Florida's American Civil Liberties Union (ACLU), Gill took his case to court. Child psychology experts testified that there was no scientific evidence that would support the state's ban on gay adoption, and that it would be in the children's best interests if they stayed with Gill and his partner. When Judge Lederman ruled the state ban unconstitutional and granted adoption rights to Gill, the case was seen as a huge milestone for gay and lesbian prospective parents in Florida, and for LGBT [lesbian, gay, bisexual, and transgender] rights activists worldwide. The attorney general's office, however, filed an appeal minutes after the decision. The case is now [as of November 2009] pending in the Third District Court of Appeals, leaving the Gill family waiting for a decision. The trial reignited a national debate surrounding gay and lesbian adoption.

Gay Adoption Has Long Been Banned in Florida

[Another family with gay parents consists of] Steven Lofton, Roger Croteau, and their children. Like Gill, they tried to fight for their right to adopt in the state of Florida. The 2005 case . . . was extremely publicized, with Rosie O'Donnell becoming one of their many staunch supporters. The case also reached the United States Supreme Court, only to have it dismissed as a "state issue," and was sent back to the Eleventh Circuit District for further perusal.

Lofton and Croteau, both white pediatric nurses, were foster parents to HIV-positive Frank, Tracy, and Bert, who were all black, at a time in the 1980s when people were hesitant and scared of those afflicted with HIV/AIDS. The children have been with Lofton and Croteau since they were infants. Bert had been in their care since he was 2 months old; at age 3, he had seroreverted [spontaneously lost HIV-specific antibodies] and tested negative for HIV. Once free from the virus, Bert was considered to be more adoptable. The state of Florida put him up for adoption, but refused Lofton's request to adopt Bert because of the state ban on gay adoption. The family

then moved to Oregon on the premise that Florida would release the children to Oregon's state laws—until Florida decided to keep the three children as its wards.

Michel Horvat, a family friend and director of the Lofton-
Croteau documentary *We Are Dad*, chronicled the family's
struggle for equal rights in adopting Bert, and the social stigma
that ensued. Shot in a span of four years, the documentary
closely followed the Lofton-Croteau family in their everyday
routine. It also showed the underlying tension between the
state of Florida and the family, even though they moved to
Oregon, where they eventually adopted two other HIV-positive
children, Wayne and Ernie, now 16 and 13. "I made a film
about their lives to let the world know who these people were,"
says Horvat. "They were a representation of a much bigger
struggle that was going on."

Although the Lofton-Croteau family is filled with love and
mutual respect, a number of organizations decried the couple
being adoptive parents, fearing for the safety and stability of
the children. In truth, the family is like any heterosexual
household; the parents drive their children to school, help
them with their homework, ask them to help with the laundry, encourage volunteer work, and support them in their ex-
tracurricular activities. . . .

Studies Support Gay Adoption

While there are promising changes in the way gay adoption is
being viewed and practiced, many people are still staunchly
opposed to it. In the Gill and Lofton cases, organizations like
the Liberty Counsel, American College of Pediatricians, and
the Christian Coalition [of America] expressed reservations in
court about allowing gay and lesbian people to adopt. Lawyers
and experts of the state in the case against Gill presented reasons why children would be considered in danger if placed
with gay or lesbian parents. They said that homosexuality
would attract unnecessary social stigma to the children and

that, scientifically, children could become homosexuals as well. Furthermore, they said that homosexual relationships were oftentimes unstable and insecure, thus likely prompting depression.

CWLA filed amicus briefs for both Lofton's and Gill's cases, citing that the ban on gay adoptive parents goes against well-established child welfare policies, saying every prospective family must be screened on an individual basis, to make sure they match the needs of the child. CWLA's position statement with regard to gay and lesbian adoption reads that "lesbian, gay, and bisexual parents are as well suited to raise children as their heterosexual counterparts." CWLA believes that by excluding gays and lesbians from the prospective resource parent pool, some children will not be afforded the privilege of having a permanent home. In 2008, there were 130,000 children waiting to be adopted, according to the [U.S] Children Bureau's "Trends in Foster Care and Adoption" report. Children waiting to be adopted were defined as those children with a goal of adoption and those whose parental rights were terminated.

Studies conducted by other experts have also countered the arguments of those opposed to gay adoption. Dr. Frederick Berlin, associate professor at the Johns Hopkins University School of Medicine, testified in Gill's case against Florida. He says that with regard to children becoming gay because of having gay parents, "there is no evidence whatsoever to support that. If the sexual orientation of the parents was what would determine the sexual orientation of the children, then presumably we won't have so many gay children growing up in heterosexual homes."

Berlin stresses that based on decades' worth of studies, the parents' sexual orientation does not determine the sexual orientation of the child. "Anytime a child can grow up in a home where they have the love of parents ... and can guide them and help them get off to a good start in life, that can be a good thing ... whether in a homosexual environment or a heterosexual environment," he says.

Dr. Stephen Erich, an associate professor in the University of Houston-Clear Lake, also did extensive research on the topic. His two-decade study on gay parents and their children is consistent with Berlin's studies and concludes that there is no empirical evidence that would suggest that children growing up with gay parents would negatively impact their well-being. By conducting research on children ages 6 and 7, and on adolescents, Erich observed a myriad of variables that would help determine the state of the household. He studied the parent's ability to get support from the community, family functioning, and the behavior of the children, among others. The study concluded that the children were doing well and that the parents were able to sustain effective support networks. His study on 154 adoptive families and 210 adolescents yielded the same positive results. The teenagers were equally attached to their parents, whether they were gay or heterosexual. . . .

Gay Families Have Much in Common with Traditional Families

The Milanos have always been dedicated and supportive parents, but they weren't without their share of raised eyebrows and prodding looks. "We got more stuff like that when [Ruben] was a baby," Stephen says. People had tried to make sense of Stephen and Joe's relationship when they were out with their sons, often staring and wondering if they were friends, or uncles, or something more, but overall they have not received extremely disparaging criticism. They are well acquainted with people in their area, and know all the other parents in the community. Stephen admits that there have been people in their sons' school who have tried to steer clear from them, but he doesn't let it affect their family.

Growing Support for Gay Adoption

Shifting views on homosexual policies

Allowing gay adoption	1999 %	2006 %
Favor	38	46
Oppose	57	48
Don't know	5	6
	100	100

Gays serving openly in military	1994 %	2006 %
Favor	52	60
Oppose	45	32
Don't know	3	8
	100	100

TAKEN FROM: "Less Opposition to Gay Marriage, Adoption and Military Service," The Pew Research Center for the People and the Press, March 22, 2006.

Their sons have begun to notice that their family is different from that of their classmates. Stephen explains to his children that every family is different, saying that one family has only one mom, another has just one dad, while another has a stepmom and another has a stepdad. Once, in kindergarten, Ruben's friend noticed that he had two fathers. Parents usually drop their children off at school, and upon seeing his fathers, Ruben's friend asked, "So, you have two dads?" Ruben said yes.

"No moms?" his friend prodded. Ruben said yes a second time.

"Cool!" the friend happily exclaimed.

The Milanos are like any other traditional family, in that they share a sense of respect and love for each other. They believe it's not a question of who comprises the family, but a question of the value and depth of the relationships among the family members.

As for Gill, he is hoping every day that he'll be allowed to keep his own family together. His case still sits in appeal, and the court posts its decisions online every Wednesday morning. "We're just sitting here waiting. Any Wednesday at 10:30 [a.m.] ... we could get a decision, in a month or three months," Gill says. "I noticed on Wednesday mornings my behavior's a little different. At first I didn't know why, but I'm walking on pins and needles all Wednesday morning. After 10:30, I realize why."

"There is not enough sound statistical evidence about children raised by single-sex caregivers to determine definitively what long-term effects this arrangement will have. Still, what evidence does exist gives serious cause for concern."

Gay Adoption Should Not Be Permitted

Thomas D. Williams

Thomas D. Williams, a Catholic priest, is dean of the theology school at Rome's Pontifical Regina Apostolorum University and serves as a Vatican analyst for NBC News and MSNBC.

In the following viewpoint, Williams defends the position of Boston's Catholic Charities in its refusal to place children with same-sex couples. All adoption agencies use criteria for the purposes of evaluating potential parents, he states. Williams argues that—while there is insufficient evidence to categorically state whether or not children raised in same-sex families suffer emotionally—there is data that exists indicating these children have

Father Thomas D. Williams, "Let Catholic Charities Be Catholic," *National Review Online*, March 21, 2006, Copyright © 2006 by National Review, Inc., 215 Lexington Avenue, New York, NY 10016. Reproduced by permission.

issues with gender identity. Given these concerns, it is appropriate for Catholic Charities to use heterosexuality as a criterion for adoption, asserts Williams.

As you read, consider the following questions:

1. According to the author, what are some of the ways in which the commonwealth of Massachusetts discriminates against certain people who wish to adopt?

2. What are some of the benefits that the author finds of families consisting of a mother and a father?

3. How does the author refute the argument that allowing gays to adopt is better than an alternative of having many unadoptable children?

Much fuss is being made over Boston's Catholic Charities' refusal to place children with same-sex couples in its adoption services. The political agenda behind the garment-rending and name-calling should have more than Catholics up in arms.

Let me start by saying that I wouldn't expect everyone to agree with the criteria employed by Catholic Charities in its selection process. After all, the Church attempts to find a home that provides not only material comfort, but also a morally and spiritually sound environment according to its own standards and perspective. A living arrangement that the Church considers to be objectively sinful doesn't qualify as being in children's best interests. But no one is required to make use of the Catholic agency, and plenty of other options exist for those who disagree.

All Adoptions Use Criteria for Parental Selection

What I would strenuously resist is an attempt to make religiously inspired or private agencies conform to a one-size-fits-all, state-imposed model of parental selection. The Christian Church has been looking after widows, orphans, and the destitute since long before the U.S. federal government came into existence. Why should a secular model trump other legitimate standards for adoption? Isn't that, after all, why a variety of adoption agencies came into existence—to provide parents with options that correspond to their values and concerns? In what way does a *de facto* [in reality] secular monopoly serve the common good better than a range of adoption alternatives?

Let's cut through the rhetoric of "discrimination" that only clouds the issue. The simple fact is that *all* adoption agencies discriminate—that is the purpose of the evaluation of prospective parents. Candidates must run a grueling gauntlet of tests, interviews, and questionnaires covering everything from their financial situation to their personal histories, education and criminal record. The commonwealth of Massachusetts applies any number of litmus tests to weed out unsuitable candidates. Let's just take the example of financial discrimination. The poor may not adopt. In order to adopt, couples must not only demonstrate economic solvency, but wealth. I personally know of several loving, married, middle-class couples that have been denied adoption simply because their bank account wasn't big enough. The question then becomes, not whether agencies should discriminate, but rather, on what grounds they should discriminate.

Catholic Charities believes that same-sex caregivers do not provide an atmosphere that is conducive to the well-rounded rearing of children. Despite all the talk of generic "parenting," mothers and fathers are not androgynous, interchangeable "parental units." A mother is not expendable and cannot be replaced by a second father. When she is missing, something essential is lost. To deliberately deprive a child of a mother or a father is to do violence to that child. Moreover, not only are both parents necessary for the unique contribution each provides, they also furnish an example of interaction between the sexes themselves.

Children Deserve a Mother and a Father

There is not enough sound statistical evidence about children raised by single-sex caregivers to determine definitively what long-term effects this arrangement will have. Still, what evidence does exist gives serious cause for concern. Most studies suggest that mothers' and fathers' complementary input aids in a child's psycho-sexual development, and studies show that children raised by single-sex caregivers have a much higher rate of gender dissatisfaction.

Again, none of it (and there's more) is conclusive, but it does illustrate the reasonableness of the position taken by Catholic Charities. Adoption agencies exist in order to help children, not to subject them to experiments in progressive social engineering whose long-term effects are not certain. Where serious doubt exists, prudence would dictate following the less risky path.

Some have countered that entrusting children to gay couples, while perhaps not the best option, beats the alternatives. There simply are not enough available married couples willing to adopt, and gays fill the gap. Yet this logic is based on two false premises. First, there are long lines of married couples waiting to adopt a child, many of whom spend years navigating the labyrinthine adoption process. Most often, what are lacking are not adoptive parents, but children to adopt. The process can become so frustrating and drawn out that many opt for other alternatives, like adopting a child from a foreign country. Second, where gay adoption is permitted, no special rules apply granting preference to married couples, and children are placed indiscriminately with homosexual couples and heterosexuals. Once again, the determining factor often becomes income, as if a plasma television, MP3 player, and Game Boy were more important for a child than a mother and father.

Finally, the adoption issue has often been mistakenly identified as a question of gay rights. Yet children are not a commodity that all should "have," and no one has the *right* to adopt. Children do, however, have the right to a mother and a father. Adoption is not about filling an emotional void in adults' lives, but offering a stable home to unfortunate children. When political agendas prevail over the best interests of children, sloppy moral reasoning is sure to follow.

Adoption reform is long overdue, and much bureaucratic dead wood needs to be hewn out of the adoption process. Yet this reform must be carried out in a way that favors the physical, emotional, and spiritual needs of children. If Catholic Charities chooses to raise the bar a little higher, they should be congratulated rather than vilified.

> *"No matter how you deconstruct the feelings involved, surrogacy contracts create babies on demand, often babies for profit."*

Surrogate Mothers Have the Right to Seek Custody

Lorraine Dusky

Lorraine Dusky is a writer who gave up her daughter many years ago in a closed adoption in New York.

In the following viewpoint, Dusky applauds the decision of a New Jersey judge upholding the custody rights of a surrogate mother. In similar situations—including the landmark case of Baby M, in which the surrogate mother carried her own genetic child for a couple, and then decided she wanted to keep the baby—Dusky contends that the press generally favors the side of the adoptive parents. Birth mothers are often discriminated against because of class prejudices, Dusky argues.

As you read, consider the following questions:

1. What reasons did the judge give for allowing Mary Beth Whitehead, the surrogate mother in the Baby M case, access to the child?

Lorraine Dusky, "Surrogate Mother Wins Right to Sue for Custody; Police Chief Sentenced for Stealing Surrogate Items," Birth Mother, First Mother Forum, December 31, 2009. Reproduced by permission of the author.

2. What were some of the reasons Dusky cites to prove that the press favored the adoptive couple over the surrogate mother in the Baby M case?

3. What reasons does the author give to support her argument against surrogate pregnancies?

In the world of convoluted conception, complications are setting in like labor pains—they are not going away anytime soon. On the heels of yesterday's [December 30, 2009's] post about a biological mother going underground with her daughter rather than sharing the girl as court ordered with her former gay partner and legal parent, today there's another surrogacy custody fight heading for the courts in the spring.

A Surrogate Mother Wins Right to Sue for Custody

A New Jersey judge has ruled that a surrogate mother who bore twin girls not conceived with her ova is the legal mother of the children and has the right to seek primary custody of them at trial in the spring. The woman, Angelia G. Robinson of Jersey City, agreed to bear the children for her brother, Donald Robinson Hollingsworth, and his male spouse, Sean Hollingsworth, using Sean's—not her brother's—sperm. After the girls were born in October 2006, they went to live with the men, but within six months, in March 2007, Robinson sought custody, alleging that she had been coerced into the arrangement. Since then she has been taking care of the girls three days a week.

Judge Francis B. Schultz of Superior Court relied heavily on precedent established by the New Jersey Superior Court in the infamous 1987–88 case of Baby M, in which a surrogate mother, Mary Beth Whitehead, carried her own genetic child for another couple, Elizabeth and William Stern, after being artificially inseminated with Stern's sperm. After she gave birth, Whitehead breastfed the baby and decided she could

Copyright © 2002 by Mike Keefe and CagleCartoons.com. All rights reserved.

not give her up. In the end, in a legally complicated and convoluted decision, the Sterns were granted custody, but the court ruled that Whitehead's maternal rights could not be terminated against her will, *that surrogacy contracts were against public policy*. Whitehead was eventually able to win visitation rights, and though I can't find them on the Net today, I remember reading at least one story several years later when the girl was visiting Whitehead and her two half-siblings at her home.

The Case of Baby M Showed Bias of the Media

At the time, both the adoption *and* adoption-reform community were deeply involved in the ongoing saga that generated nearly as many stories in the media as a certain famous golfer with a predilection for promiscuity did recently. Though the adoption-reform community came down heavily in favor of giving Whitehead custody of her daughter, most of the rest of the media tilted toward the Sterns. Working-class Whitehead was portrayed as a somewhat pathetic creature—she was unstable because she changed her mind about giving up her daughter—and the expert testimony at trial was heavily weighted in favor of the upstanding middle-class couple, the Sterns. For having agreed to be a surrogate in the first place, for not being of the solid middle-class background of the Sterns (Elizabeth Stern was a doctor), for having the temerity to change her mind about giving up her baby, Whitehead was pilloried in the press. However, there were exceptions.

We note that one of our friends, Michelle Harrison, now an adoptive mother to many in India—not from, but IN India—wrote in *Perspectives* that the testimony of experts was heavily "imbued with prevailing middle-class beliefs about good mothers and good parenting." Which of course would exclude many first/birth mothers—then, and today—from being considered suitable mothers. The *New York Times* ran an editorial, "There Is Nothing Surrogate About the Pain," that condemned the trial as biased against both women and the working class and called for joint custody. Feminists, who have largely looked away from the plight of first/birth mothers, spoke out for Whitehead. Adoption-reform pioneer Florence Fisher did also.

Yet the prevailing wind was with the Sterns. Even most women, without the perspective of having lost a child to adoption, or in a custody fight, sided with the couple. They simply did not like lower-class Mary Beth. Feminist thinker and author Phyllis Chesler took up Whitehead's cause and wrote in *Sacred Bond, The Legacy of Baby M*: "Women who have never been allowed to talk back eventually identify with the aggressor and have no pity for a victim who reminds them of themselves." To which we add: Amen.

It is worth noting here that Mrs. Stern was not infertile but had multiple sclerosis, and was concerned about the possible physical implications of pregnancy. A colleague testified that his wife, with the same condition, had temporary paralysis during pregnancy. Incidentally, the contract between Whitehead and the Sterns is available online. She was to be paid $10,000 for a live infant. It's really kinda awful to read, and certainly considers the baby as property.

Surrogacy Contracts Ignore the Best Interests of the Child

While the Baby M case did uphold the surrogacy contract, the judgment was not laudatory about the arrangement, and the judge in the current case in New Jersey (what is it about New Jersey, is it something in the water?) quoted this in the current decision:

> "The surrogacy contract," the Baby M court found, "is based on principles that are directly contrary to the objectives of our laws. It guarantees the separation of a child from its mother; it looks to adoption regardless of suitability; it totally ignores the child; it takes the child from the mother regardless of her wishes and maternal fitness."

Citing that passage, Judge Schultz wrote, "Would it really make any difference if the word 'gestational' was substituted for the word 'surrogacy' in the above quotation? I think not."

All this reminds us once again why we do not like surrogacy pregnancies—with the woman's own eggs, or with another woman's eggs. No matter how you deconstruct the feelings involved, surrogacy contracts create babies on demand, often babies for profit. We ask, how different is the situation of a surrogate mother different from a first/birth mother who agrees to sign—or does sign—papers relinquishing her child but changes her mind hours, days, weeks later? Does the fact that the birth began with a surrogacy contract make the experience different?

We think not. Having given up a child of our own egg, we do think there may be an emotional difference between a purely gestational surrogate mother and a genetic mother, but we do not have the answers today, and nor are we even sure of our feelings.

"Surrogate mothers who are not genetically related to the child have had little
success in obtaining any kind of parental rights."

Surrogate Mothers Have No Right to Seek Custody

Brian Palmer

Brian Palmer is a writer living in New York City.

The twin babies born in June 2009 to a mother acting as a surrogate for actors Sarah Jessica Parker and Matthew Broderick brought the issues surrounding surrogacy into the news. The laws concerning surrogacy are a work in progress and vary from state to state, Palmer reports. However, in general, if the eggs of the surrogate are not used, the surrogate mother has no claim to custody. Palmer contends that contracts between the intended parents and birth mothers can be enormously complex.

As you read, consider the following questions:

1. What are some of the different steps toward establishing legal parenthood in various states following a surrogate birth?

Brian Palmer, "Will Sarah Jessica Parker's Surrogate Get Visitation Rights?" *Slate*, June 25, 2009. www.slate.com, Copyright © 2009 The Slate Group. All rights reserved. Used by permission and protected by the Copyright Laws of the United States. The printing, copying, redistribution or retransmission of the Material without express written permission is prohibited.

2. What steps does the author recommend for intended parents in order to avoid complications?

3. What are some of the lifestyle aspects covered in many surrogate contracts?

A surrogate mother gave birth to twin girls for actors Matthew Broderick and Sarah Jessica Parker in Ohio on Monday [June 22, 2009]. The celebrity parents are ready to take the newborns home and leave the birth mother in the Rust Belt. Does the surrogate have any rights now that the children are born?

Surrogacy Law Is Complex and Unsettled

Not if they used Parker's eggs. Surrogate mothers who are not genetically related to the child have had little success in obtaining any kind of parental rights. But surrogacy is an enormously complicated and unsettled area of law, and different states take different approaches. In surrogacy-friendly states, like Ohio and California, a judge issues an order, either before or immediately after the delivery, recognizing the genetic parents as the legal guardians, and directs the hospital to do the same. As part of the process, the surrogate normally waives any right to contest custody. In other states, the intended mother may have to go through an adoption procedure. Still, as long as the surrogate is on board, any state will eventually grant custody to the intended parents. Once legal parenthood is established, the surrogate has no legal relationship to the child—not even visitation rights.

In the event of a renegade surrogate or divorce of the intended parents, things can get very messy. This is where planning is important. If possible, couples should never use the surrogate mother's egg, as this arrangement strengthens her claim to parental rights. If the intended mother's eggs aren't viable, smart couples use a third-party egg donor. Second, choice of state is crucial. Surrogacy is actually a crime in Ari-

Surrogacy Is a Murky Legal Area

Surrogacy is a complicated subject, to say the least. It involves many of the issues central to reproductive justice—bodily autonomy, a woman's right to abortion, definitions of parenthood, and custody of children. It's also an option increasingly relied upon by gay couples—usually gay men—to create families. It invariably brings up concerns about racial and economic justice when the majority of surrogates are low income and many are women of color. It's an issue on which few reproductive rights and justice groups are currently working but one that deserves our close attention.

Miriam Pérez, "Surrogacy:
The Next Frontier for Reproductive Justice,"
RHRealityCheck.org, February 23, 2010.

zona (although the law has not been enforced), and some states, like North Dakota, don't recognize surrogacy agreements at all. In these states, if the intended parents divorce and start bickering over custody, the surrogacy contract is worthless, and family law statutes come into play. Depending on the jurisdiction, courts may then simply presume that the birth mother is the legal mother—and her husband the father—and it's up to the intended parents to overcome that presumption in a lengthy court battle while the birth mother raises the child.

Contracts Cover Multiple Situations

The surrogacy contract, often around 40 pages, governs much more than just custody. It requires in-depth psychological testing of the mother to make sure she is emotionally prepared to carry out her duties (including giving up the baby) as well as STD [sexually transmitted disease] tests and other physical exams. Once the pregnancy commences, the contract can dictate many aspects of the surrogate's life. Drinking, smoking, and risky behaviors like skydiving are invariably prohibited. The contract can also require the surrogate to eat a generically healthy diet, or it can go so far as to mandate an organic-only diet.

Then there are the stickier issues: money and abortion. The intended parents pay all medical expenses if the surrogate's insurer balks. They also send a monthly check to the surrogate to cover expenses like vitamins and trips to the doctor as well as the agreed-upon compensation. The going rate is between $20,000 and $30,000 spread over the course of the pregnancy. (In the event of a miscarriage, the surrogate usually keeps what she has received by the time of the termination.) The contract will also dictate whether an abortion is in order should testing reveal certain problems with the fetus.

Similarly, the mother may be required to have an abortion in the event of multiple fetuses—a common event in surrogacy. But the contract may be worthless paper in this sensitive area. It is highly unlikely that a court would force a woman to have an abortion, and there is no case law on what happens if the surrogate refuses to carry the baby to term even though the contract requires it.

> "Within a week of bringing them home, we contacted our adoption agency and told them our experience was very different from what we had expected."

Sometimes Adopted Children Must Be Returned to the State's Care

Josephine A. Ruggiero

Josephine A. Ruggiero is the author of Eastern European Adoption: Policies, Practice, and Strategies for Change.

Although this is not a desirable outcome, there are instances when adoptive parents return children to the care of the state for inpatient treatment or placement in a foster home. In the following viewpoint, Josephine A. Ruggiero discusses the case of an adoptive family who sent their seven-year-old boy back to Russia. Despite the negative reactions presented by the media, Ruggiero empathizes with the adoptive family. Along with her husband, Ruggiero adopted three biological siblings from Russia, who suffered from serious medical and emotional issues, such as post-traumatic stress disorder and fetal alcohol syndrome. Adoption agencies, Ruggiero asserts, should have better post-adoptive services for extreme situations.

Josephine A. Ruggiero, "When Adoption Isn't Easy," *Newsweek*, April 15, 2010. Reproduced by permission.

As you read, consider the following questions:

1. How did the adoption agency respond when contacted by the author of the viewpoint a week after the adoption?

2. What are some behavioral issues discussed by the author?

3. Name the three major challenges facing families considering Russian adoption, as listed by the author.

When I heard about the adoptive family who sent their 7-year-old boy back to Russia, I was saddened, but I wasn't surprised. They made a drastic decision, but I'm sure other adoptive parents in distress have thought about doing the very same thing.

Different than Expected

My husband and I adopted three biological siblings from Russia in 1994—a boy and two girls, all under the age of 5. We saw pictures and were assured they were healthy, but we had to make a quick decision, based on very little information. I'm trained in sociology, but nothing could have prepared me for the challenges we've encountered. The kids had serious medical and emotional issues. Both girls had some level of fetal alcohol syndrome. The youngest needed immediate surgery to repair a traumatic brain injury, and she's had seizures ever since. From the start, they all exhibited defiant behavior. Admittedly, all kids go through that phase, but we didn't expect it to happen so young. Within a week of bringing them home, we contacted our adoption agency and told them our experience was very different from what we had expected. They said something like, "We're sorry to hear that."

My husband and I spent several months with the children at home before I went back to teaching. We played with them and found Russian speakers to talk with them and read stories in Russian. The kids all suffered from post-traumatic stress disorder resulting, we believe, from neglect and both mental and physical abuse. None ever tried to hurt us, but they were unable to control their anger. It was as if they operated solely on a level of basic survival, which never seemed to be replaced by rational thinking. We had to put locks on doors inside the house, because they would take anything they wanted, including money. I'm always trying to teach them—"We don't do this in our family"—but there's no reciprocity. We once found ourselves even charged with neglect—an unsubstantiated charge that was never pursued—when our teenage son decided to live elsewhere. Every kid tries to push the limits. But most kids get it when they've pushed too far and they stop. They care about what their parents think; they love their parents. Even now, I don't see that with my children.

Major Challenges

I spent more than a decade researching Russian adoption, and I believe families face three major challenges. First, they are not adequately prepared in the pre-adoption phase for the kinds of emotional struggles their children might face. Second, they often receive incomplete or even false medical and background information. Third, there is a lack of post-adoptive services specializing in behavioral issues. Ultimately, I believe everybody would benefit if adoptees were placed in foster care in their home countries before joining families in the United States. Children need a transition period after life in an orphanage; they need to get a sense of what the give-and-take of family life is all about.

Most Russian adoptions are successful. In our case, we kept thinking that our kids' early behavioral issues stemmed from the challenges of adjusting to their new life. But they only got worse. My youngest, who's 17, still gets very defensive and starts screaming. I can't say I have any real relationship with my older daughter, 19, much as I'd like to. My son, 20, lives on his own and doesn't communicate with us. It's awfully hard to take strangers and try to make them into people who love you. There isn't any doubt that we love them, but I think it's hard for them to understand what love means.

My children are a success as far as society goes. My son's in college; my older daughter hopes to go in the fall. They're polite, friendly, and respectful—just not with us. We continue to love our children through all of it. It's like climbing a mountain, but we haven't reached the top, where it gets easier. I'm thinking that may never happen.

"No matter what the real situation was—and who knows how much of the actual story we will ever know—givebacks aren't an option."

Returning Adopted Children Is Never an Option

Joanne Bamberger

Joanne Bamberger is a writer and political and media analyst based in Washington, D.C. Her work has appeared in many publications, including the Washington Post *and* Adoptive Families *magazine.*

On April 8, 2010, adoptive mother Torry Hansen put her son, Artyom, unaccompanied, on a flight back to his native Russia, claiming the child was mentally unstable, and she was no longer able to care for him. As a mother by adoption of a daughter from China, Bamberger finds Hansen's action inexcusable. No child is perfect, writes Bamberger in the following viewpoint, and all parents have to deal with some issues for which they aren't prepared. Whether a child is biological, adopted, foster, or born through a surrogacy arrangement, all have issues of varying

Joanne Bamberger, "Children Don't Come with Return Policies," The Stir, April 13, 2010. Reproduced by permission.

degrees of seriousness. Responsible parents find resources to help their child and themselves; returning a child should never be an option, Bamberger argues.

As you read, consider the following questions:

1. Bamberger is the mother of an adopted child from China. What are some of the adjustment issues her daughter faced?

2. What are some of the factors in Artyom's background that the author concedes could have caused emotional issues?

3. What are some of the negative fallouts that the author fears could result from this high-profile failed adoption?

Close your eyes and imagine this—you are seven years old. Your mother, one you have only known six months, puts you on a 15-hour flight by yourself with a bunch of strangers whose language you barely understand. You fly all day to get to a place where no one is waiting for you because no one knows you are coming. And you probably don't know this yet, but you're not even a citizen of that country anymore. You get off the plane and have to explain to yet another stranger what's just happened. You probably start to cry.

Most of us don't have too many vivid memories from when we were seven years old, but I have a feeling that young Artyom, aka Justin Hansen, will relive that memory for the rest of his life.

I am a mother by adoption, so you can probably guess that I have a LOT to say about Artyom, the Russian adoptee who his mother claims was threatening to burn down her house and was becoming violent.

I don't doubt any of that. All children have issues of one kind or another—some mild, some extremely serious. And there are some that come up more often in adopted children, like attachment issues, than in our children who come to us the "old-fashioned" way. But as I like to say, there are no "givebacks" when it comes to children, no matter how they become part of our families.

My husband and I adopted our daughter from China nine years ago. . . . She was 12 months old at the time, and we knew there was a possibility that we would have to deal with attachment or emotional issues because she lived in an orphanage for a year. The orphanage caregivers we met seemed like nice women who genuinely cared about the babies, but there were eight of them and 100 babies to take care of every day. With that kind of ratio, it's no surprise that some children who come out of that experience have a tough time building trust in their new parents and believing that these new people will love them and care for them and never leave them.

We hoped that wouldn't be the case but, as it turned out, we spent a long time working on attachment, bonding and trust issues with our daughter. As a somewhat typical fourth grader today, PunditGirl is doing well now, but it never crossed our minds to put her on a plane back to China when the going got rough.

I wrote about this a few months ago when another mother, who had five biological children, adopted a sixth and then gave him up because of emotional issues and bonding problems. I wrote then about our own experience:

> We thought we were prepared. We dealt with a fabulous agency who made sure we knew that a good number of children adopted from institutions often have attachment and other emotional issues. We read. We listened. We talked. MY husband already had experience as a dad to two biological daughters. We thought we were ready.

> We so weren't.

But the thing is this—no one is EVER ready for the parenting experience they get, whether their children are biological,

Alternatives Existed

"This woman had alternatives," says Debbie Spivack, an adoption attorney with offices in Pennsylvania, New Jersey and Delaware who has helped facilitate placement of children given up by their adoptive families [referring to Torry Hansen, a woman in Tennessee who put her seven-year-old adopted son back on a plane to Russia alone after she found she could not deal with his emotional/behavioral issues]. "She really endangered the child and did something exceptionally damaging for everybody else."

Kate Pickert,
"Russian Adoption: What Happens When a Parent Gives Up,"
Time, April 14, 2010.

adopted, foster or the result of today's myriad fertility options that may or may not result in a child that's biologically related to the ultimate parents. No one is ever really ready for a child with autism, Down syndrome, cancer, diabetes, ADHD [attention deficit hyperactivity disorder]—no child is perfect and every parenting experience is different, yet most of us find ways to rise to the occasion and help our children the best we can.

Given what I know about international adoption, I have no doubt that young Artyom had serious emotional issues—he was a seven-year-old living in an institution and had been placed there by an alcoholic mother. He told stories of being beaten with a broom in the orphanage (a story apparently other children from Russian orphanages have told, as well). I have no doubt that he threatened to set the family home on fire or threatened other violence, because I have heard that story before in connection with older institutionalized children who were later adopted. I have no doubt that the whole truth wasn't told by the orphanage. And I have no doubt that perhaps the family didn't get or hear the whole message from the adoption agency they used about the potential serious emotional and behavior issues a child like Artyom might have.

But there are resources. And there is help. That's what all the follow-up placement services are there for. No matter what the real situation was—and who knows how much of the actual story we will ever know—givebacks aren't an option.

I am sad for the other families who are waiting to adopt their children from Russia who are now in indefinite limbo as a result of this. And I'm sad for all adoptive families, including mine, who get painted with the broad brush of media judgment because families by adoption are still considered second-best in our country and scrutinized in ways that other families aren't. But most of all, I'm sad for Artyom and hope that something in his life will start to go right very soon.

> "We are not suggesting that the child's views should be the deciding factor, but that the court must know the child's views and that the child must know that her views are a part of the process."

Children Should Have a Voice in Determining Their Own Custody

Family Law Quarterly

Family Law Quarterly *is a scholarly journal covering legal aspects of family life.*

Approximately 120,000 children are adopted annually in the United States and another 700,000 have their guardianship determined every year. Although the decisions surrounding adoption and guardianship will profoundly affect these children for their entire lives, very few children have a voice in these decisions, according to the authors in the following viewpoint. While there are differing means in various states to solicit the input of

"Hearing Children's Voices and Interests in Adoption and Guardianship Proceedings," *Family Law Quarterly*, vol. 41, no. 2. © Copyright 2008 by the American Bar Association. Reprinted with permission. This information or any or portion thereof may not be copied or disseminated in any form or by any means or stored in an electronic database or retrieval system without the express written consent of the American Bar Association.

the child in custody decisions—such as through the appointment of an advocate—there is no consistent, adequate approach. The authors contend that in all instances where the child is not an infant, it is the responsibility of the court to arrange for the child to have the process explained to him or her and to have the opportunity to voice an opinion that receives consideration.

As you read, consider the following questions:

1. What were the recommendations of the Pew Commission on Children in Foster Care in its 2004 report?

2. What are some of the limitations the authors point to in the use of advocates in adoption and guardianship cases?

3. While many states require the child's consent to adoption or guardianship, this requirement is often a meaningless formality, according to the authors. What reasons do they give for their opinion?

More than 120,000 children are adopted annually in the United States, and approximately 700,000 are the subject of a proceeding to determine who will be their guardian. These life-altering decisions have an enormous impact on children. Yet more often than not, the concerns and voices of the children themselves are neither elicited nor obtained. In some instances, it may be impossible to hear from a child or her advocate. In many situations, however, hearing from the child or his legal representative will be essential to making the best decisions for the child, to respecting the child, and to recognizing that it is the child who is at the center of an otherwise disempowering process. . . .

In 2003, the Pew Commission on Children in Foster Care, a national, nonpartisan panel funded by the Pew Charitable Trusts, conducted a comprehensive assessment of the federal financing system as well as the court structure responsible for oversight of cases involving abuse, neglect, and dependency.

While the commission was seated and conducted its deliberations, Fostering Results began its work both at the national level and in selected states to highlight the need to address the role of federal financing as well as the role of the courts in foster cases.

In May of 2004, the Pew Commission released its recommendations and for the first time, a national study and report placed equal weight on the role of the court and the role of the agency in handling child welfare cases. Half of the Pew Commission recommendations came under the goal of "Strengthening Courts." In the prefatory comments, the commission stated that "no child ... should face the partial or permanent severance of familial ties without a fully informed voice in the legal process." The commission also recognized that courts have enormous responsibility in the dependency area and are making decisions without children having a strong and effective voice. Formal Recommendation 3 states:

> To safeguard children's best interests in dependency court proceedings, children ... must have a direct voice in court, effective representation, and the timely input of those who care about them. . . .

Consideration of Child's Preference in Adoption Proceedings

Today fifty jurisdictions employ statutory language directing the court to consider in some capacity a child's preferences during adoption proceedings. Forty-nine jurisdictions require courts to contemplate a child's preferences by requiring a child's consent for the adoption if a child has attained a certain age. The jurisdictions that require a child's consent for adoption use the threshold age of ten, twelve, or fourteen. Twenty-five jurisdictions require consent if an adoptee is either fourteen or older; eighteen jurisdictions use age twelve or older; six jurisdictions use age ten or older.

Even jurisdictions that require a child's consent to an adoption if the child is above a certain age allow courts the discretion to dispense with consent requirements. For example, many jurisdictions explicitly allow courts to dispense with the consent requirement if doing so is in a child's best interests, or, as in West Virginia, for "extraordinary cause." One legislature reasoned that the flexibility in allowing courts to eliminate the consent requirement might serve a child's best interests in certain types of cases, for example, where a child who does not know of his or her status as a stepchild or of the pending adoption proceedings or where he or she is being adopted by a stepparent.

Although a majority of jurisdictions direct courts to consider a child's preferences in adoption proceedings through consent requirements, seven jurisdictions guide courts to consider a child's preferences in other ways. Colorado has a rebuttable presumption that relinquishment is not in an adoptee's best interests if a child is twelve or older and objects, and requires written consent to any adoption for a child twelve or older. New Jersey requires the child to appear at the final adoption hearing and directs courts to solicit a child's wishes regarding the adoption, provided that a child has the capacity to form an intelligent preference with regard to the adoption, unless good cause is shown. Alaska directs courts to consider a child's wishes even if an adoptee is under the age at which his or her consent is required, provided that a child has sufficient age and intelligence to state his or her preferences regarding the adoption. Colorado and Oregon specifically provide the court may talk with the child. Missouri and Oklahoma include ascertaining the child's wishes in the duties of the guardian ad litem. Michigan, which makes no reference to the appointment of a representative for the child, does provide that the court shall consider the child's preference if the adoptee is fourteen or younger and the court considers the adoptee to be of sufficient age to express a preference. Finally,

Foster Care Population by State, (FY 2004)

State	# of Children in Foster Care	State	# of Children in Foster Care
Alabama	5,880	Montana	2,030
Alaska	1,825	Nebraska	6,292
Arizona	9,119	Nevada	4,050
Arkansas	3,097	New Hampshire	1,236
California	92,344	New Jersey	12,702
Colorado	8,196	New Mexico	2,150
Connecticut	6,803	New York	33,445
Delaware	849	North Carolina	10,007
Florida	28,864	North Dakota	1,314
Georgia	14,216	Ohio	18,004
Hawaii	2,953	Oklahoma	10,572
Idaho	1,565	Oregon	10,096
Illinois	19,931	Pennsylvania	21,944
Indiana	9,745	Rhode Island	2,414
Iowa	5,384	South Carolina	4,855
Kansas	6,060	South Dakota	1,600
Kentucky	7,000	Tennessee	9,590
Louisiana	4,397	Texas	24,529
Maine	2,584	Utah	2,108
Maryland	11,111	Vermont	1,432
Massachusetts	12,562	Virginia	6,869
Michigan	21,173	Washington	9,368
Minnesota	7,038	West Virginia	3,990
Mississippi	2,989	Wisconsin	7,812
Missouri	11,681	Wyoming	1,209
		National	**507,054**

TAKEN FROM: PewFosterCare.org, 2004.

in recent years, a number of states have added provisions in their adoption laws that deal with post-adoption contact. Provisions in nine states require consideration of the child's wishes on the issues of post-adoption contact, either by requiring the child's consent or consideration of the child's wishes.

Consideration of Child's Preference in Guardianship Proceedings

The statutory language directing courts to consider a child's preferences during guardianship proceedings is less uniform than similar provisions within the adoption statutes. Forty-three jurisdictions employ statutory language directing courts to consider a child's preferences in guardianship proceedings. A majority of jurisdictions establish a threshold age when courts are required to consider a child's preferences, but much variance exists in how courts are required to consider a child's wishes. In addition, the courts have broad discretion to dispense with consent requirements.

Much as a majority of adoption statutes establish a threshold age at which an adoptee's consent is required, a majority of jurisdictions require courts to consider a child's wishes in guardianship proceedings if he or she has attained a certain age. Thirty-eight jurisdictions direct courts to consider a child's preferences in some capacity if a child is either fourteen or older, three jurisdictions set the age at twelve or older. California and New Hampshire do not establish a threshold age.

Much variance exists in how statutory provisions direct courts to consider a child's preferences. For example, some statutes direct courts to appoint a guardian nominated by the child. Other statutes require courts to give preference to or consider a child's nomination of a guardian and/or the child's wishes with regard to who's appointed guardian. Others include provisions that allow a child to prevent an appointment or to terminate a previously made appointment.

Much as the adoption statutes give courts broad discretion to dispense with consideration of a child's wishes, the guardianship statutes also give courts broad discretion when considering a child's preferences. A majority of jurisdictions grant courts discretion to dispense with a child's preferences when following the child's preferences would be contrary to a child's best interests. Delaware allows courts to dispense with the requirement for the child's consent in guardianship proceedings for "just cause shown." New Hampshire, which does not establish a threshold age when courts should consider a child's preferences, directs courts to determine a child's preferences in all cases and give these preferences "such weight as under the circumstances may seem just." . . .

Children's Voices Are Heard Through Advocates

Despite the discretionary availability of advocates for children in adoption and guardianship cases, such appointments are rare and limited. Even where state statutes require appointment, the representation is often perfunctory. For example, Illinois requires appointment of a licensed attorney in every adoption case. In Cook County, Illinois, where Chicago is located, for the last several years the circuit court has appointed five attorneys to act as guardian ad litem [GAL] in all adoption cases. These attorneys work part-time while maintaining a separate private practice. In 2005, approximately 2,000 adoptions were filed in Cook County; each GAL handled approximately 400 cases. Unless the child is fourteen or the adoption is contested, the GALs generally do not interview the child. Clearly it would be extremely difficult if not impossible for GALs to come to know all of the children they are representing.

A second issue concerning the provision of advocates to children in adoption and guardianship proceedings concerns the lack of clarity as to the role of these advocates. Others have addressed the difficulties that occur due to the lack of clarity around the role and duties concerning child advocates. These issues are exacerbated in adoption and guardianship cases because the representation takes place in a statutory model that was developed when the majority of adoptees were infants and when the interests of the adoptees were considered secondary to the interests of the adopters who were seen as doing the child a favor by taking him or her into their home. Thus, the representation provided under the current system reflects the earlier view of adoption as a secret event between the biological parent and the adoptive parent with the child as an almost incidental third person, if considered individually at all.

The current system appears to incorporate the child's voice through the requirement of consent to the adoption or guardianship. Although many states theoretically provide for the child's voice through this requirement for consent, this avenue for the child's voice may be more of a mirage than a reality. First, the majority of states provide broad discretion to waive the consent. Second, only two states provide for representation for the child. Thus, children in the vast majority of states do not have any representation in presenting their voices on the question of consent. Finally, the model of adoption, which focuses on the adopting parent, the information provided by the adoption agency, and the general benefit being conveyed on the child, does not consider the individual child's voice as a significant factor.

We attempted to gather input from attorneys and judges who handle adoptions. We asked the judges about when they appoint a child advocate; when they explain the process or proceeding to the child; how the child's wishes and concerns are brought to their attention; how the child's age impacts this; what weight is given to the child's preferences; what barriers prevent getting direct information; and whether the child's concerns, wishes, and interests are adequately voiced. Unfortunately, we did not get sufficient information to draw any conclusions. What we did learn is that there is a significant lack of uniformity or concrete direction to judges as to when and how to involve children and their voices and preferences.

Children's voices currently are heard through a variety of vehicles, including the child's representative, a social worker's report, an investigator's report, and the child directly. Although some judges thought that the child's wishes and concerns are adequately brought to their attention, judges in adoption and guardianship proceedings often find that there are barriers that prevent them from ascertaining the minor's wishes, interests, and concerns.

While judges indicated that the judicial process as a whole works to allow minors' voices to be heard, they also thought certain improvements would be beneficial.

The most serious barrier is where no attorney advocate can be appointed due to cost considerations. If the judge does not interview the client on the record so that the judge knows the client's wishes, the minor's voice might not be heard. In these circumstances, situations where family conflicts are unknown to the judge might never be revealed.

Judges have found that lack of adequate counsel makes the minor an unequal player in proceedings set to determine his future. Inadequately trained or poorly qualified counsel has been a problem in adoption and guardianship proceedings.

Excessive attorney caseloads often are a barrier to minor's voices, interests, and concerns being heard. The minor is disadvantaged when his attorney advocate cannot and does not take the time to gain his trust so that he can be forthright with him about his wishes. By getting to know his client, the attorney advocate can then do any necessary investigation to fully understand his client's situation and then work with his client to present his client's wishes and the reasoning behind them to the court.

Judges expressed other factors that impede their ability to ensure the minor's wishes, concerns and interests are adequately heard in adoption and guardianship proceedings. In certain cases, there are inconveniences or delays in the judge's ability to see the children whose interests are at stake. Transportation barriers that inhibit the minor's ability to make it to court can compound these inconveniences. Even where minors can make it to court, the facilities at the court are often not conducive for the judge when he wishes to interview the minor or privately explain how the court proceedings will work. These are problems that judges wish to remedy, but which leave them wondering who will pay to make access to minors more conducive and at what cost.

Judges and attorneys are not the only major players in the adoption and guardianship proceedings. When other vital players cannot or do not perform their jobs with expertise, judicial proceedings and decisions fail to take place with well-developed facts. In some adoption and guardianship courts, there is always a court investigator or social worker to provide information to the court. When the quality and quantity of the information varies in accuracy and scope, it prevents the judge from having a complete and accurate record from which to make an informed permanency decision. . . .

Current Laws and Practices Are Inadequate to Represent Children

The current status of state law and advocacy efforts is insufficient to meet the needs of children involved in adoption and guardianship proceedings. Currently, at least one-third of the children subject to adoption, and substantially more than that in guardianship proceedings, are significantly beyond the age of infancy. The more recent understanding of adoption is of a triad involving three equal parties: the child, the biological parent(s), and the adoptive parent(s). This understanding reflects the knowledge that a family created by adoption or guardianship is not the same as a family created by birth and that the child will need to, and will, go through a process of incorporating how his family came into being. This is not a bad thing; it just is. Thus, a child's voice and feelings around adoption and guardianship are much more complicated than a mere consent or lack thereof. Their feelings and awareness around the issue of adoption or guardianship start much earlier than the ages of twelve, thirteen, or fourteen, which are most often used in statutes as the age of consent to adoption and guardianship. By the age of five a child has an awareness of and questions concerning adoption. However, on the whole, the child's voice, if heard directly, is only heard in terms of whether or not he consents to the adoption or guardianship. Additionally, the requirement of consent is almost always easily waived.

The importance of the child's understanding of the process and voice in the process is a concept that has developed and has come into its own in the last fifteen years. Significant thought has been given to the representation and needs of children in legal proceedings. The ABA [American Bar Association] Standards of Practice for Lawyers Who Represent Children in Abuse and Neglect [Cases] (1996) and the ABA Standards of Practice for Lawyers Representing Children in Custody [Cases] (2003) emphasize the need to hear the child's voice. In 2003, Pew Commission recommendations emphasized the need for a direct voice for children in decisions that impact their future. The Uniform Representation of Children in Abuse, Neglect, and Custody Proceedings Act, adopted by the National Conference of Commissioners on Uniform State Laws in July 2006 and amended in 2007, establishes the requirement that a child's voice and appropriate representation is necessary in legal proceedings that involve their custody interests.

The standard for action in adoption and guardianship proceedings, just as in dependency, is "best interest" of the child. In dependency and other types of custody proceedings in general, great strides have been made to focus on explaining the proceeding to the child and to offer the child a direct avenue to express their thoughts so that decisions are made with a detailed understanding of the child. Although a guardianship is not as permanent as an adoption, both are major decisions from a child's perspective. However, because of the old view of adoption as a secret event, the adoption and guardianship laws still fail to provide for a full understanding of the child whose life is being significantly impacted by the proceeding.

In an adoption or guardianship where the child is not an infant, the court needs to ensure that the process has been explained to the child by an appropriate party and that the child's views are reported to the court.

We are not suggesting that the child's views should be the deciding factor, but that the court must know the child's views and that the child must know that her views are a part of the process. "The child's right to be heard in any proceedings in which her custody is at stake should not be construed as a right to decide but as a right to have her views seriously considered. Such a right to be heard recognizes the child's personhood and dignity, and ensures that information of potentially unique significance will reach the court." In this way, the court will be able to hear the child's views and better ascertain whether a child's advocate is necessary and, if so, what type of representation is necessary.

Periodical and Internet Sources Bibliography

The following articles have been selected to supplement the diverse views presented in this chapter.

Lisa Belkin	"Shipping an Adopted Son Back to Russia," *New York Times*, April 9, 2010.
Kiki Dahlke	"Back in the USSR, Russian Adoption Return," Gather, April 19, 2010. http://moms.gather.com.
James C. Dobson	"Two Mommies Is One Too Many," *Time*, December 12, 2006.
Jo Knowsley	"Surrogate Mother Says 'Sorry, but I'm Keeping Your Babies,'" *Daily Mail*, December 17, 2006.
Geoff Mulvihill	"Parental Rights for Surrogate," *Philadelphia Inquirer*, January 1, 2010.
Kate Pickert	"Russian Adoption: What Happens When a Parent Gives Up?" *Time*, April 14, 2010.
Amanda Ruggeri	"Emerging Gay Adoption Fight Shares Battle Lines of Same-Sex Marriage Debate," *U.S. News & World Report*, October 31, 2008.
Maia Spotts	"When Custody Courts Fail LGBT Parents," *Gay Rights*, January 18, 2010.
Andrea Stone	"Both Sides on Gay Adoption Cite Concern for Children," *USA Today*, February 20, 2006.
Michael S. Wald	"Adults' Sexual Orientation and State Determinations Regarding Placement of Children," *Family Law Quarterly*, vol. 40, no. 3, Fall 2006.

OPPOSING
VIEWPOINTS®
SERIES

CHAPTER 3

What Is the Role of Government in Determining Child Custody?

Chapter Preface

In the United States, nearly half of all marriages end in divorce, nearly one-fourth of all children are born out of wedlock, and more than one hundred thousand children are in foster care awaiting adoption. Therefore, child custody is an important social issue and one that is usually regulated by the government at the state level. Parents are assumed to have control over all aspects of their minor children's lives. However, in cases of divorce, single parenthood, adoption, or suspected child abuse, there is sometimes a dispute over which parent, or other adult, should have responsibility for a child. In these instances, family or juvenile courts will intervene to make a decision. In the rare cases where a state law may be challenged by a custody case, an appeal can be made to the U.S. Supreme Court.

In families with children, the divorce decree typically also specifies child custody arrangements. In the vast majority of cases, parents are able to come to agreement on these matters themselves. Arrangements for child custody consist of both physical and legal custody. Physical custody is the determination of where the child will live. Physical custody can be sole custody, joint custody, or split custody—when the children of the marriage are split between the parents. Legal custody determines who has responsibility for decisions such as medical care, education, religious upbringing, and certain other matters. The most typical arrangement is for one parent to have sole physical custody with the other parent given visitation rights, but with both parents sharing legal custody.

In the approximately 10 percent of cases where the parents are unable to reach an agreement, a court will intervene, basing its decision on what is perceived to be in a child's best interests. To help determine a child's best interests, courts will often conduct custody evaluations. Some courts will appoint a third-party child's advocate to investigate and represent the best interests of the child.

In the case of unmarried parents, most states grant sole physical custody to the mother. If the father wants custody of his child, he must take a paternity test and file a petition for custody. Typically, he will receive custody only if it is determined that the mother is either unfit or unable to fulfill the role of caregiver for her child.

In the case of adoptions, most states require that both the mother and father provide their consent before a child can be adopted. Complications can arise if no father is listed on the child's birth certificate, or if the wrong father is named. Sometimes blood relatives other than a child's parents may petition for custody instead of having the child adopted or placed into foster care. In each of these instances, courts may need to intervene to make a decision in the best interest of the child.

The state also has a clearly defined role in cases where child abuse or neglect is suspected. In these instances, the investigating social services department must find "clear and compelling evidence" that it is in the best interest of the child to terminate a parent's custodial rights. When this occurs, the child can be placed with another relative, taken into foster care, or made available for adoption.

Although the state's appropriate role in determining child custody is clear in certain instances, the complexities of contemporary society have raised additional issues that fall outside the scope of existing law. In the chapter that follows, the role of government in determining child custody in complex situations is debated.

> "The purpose of this legislation is straightforward: to protect our men and women in uniform from their deployment being used against them in custody disputes."

The Child Custody Rights of Military Personnel Should Be Protected by the Federal Government

Michael R. Turner

Michael R. Turner is a Republican member of the U.S. House of Representatives from Ohio.

In the following viewpoint excerpted from a news release, Turner provides his reasons for introducing a bill to protect custody rights of members of the armed services. According to Turner, H.R. 4469 would amend the Servicemembers Civil Relief Act by protecting the custody arrangements of service members during their deployment. Additionally, the bill sought to prohibit deployment as a factor in deciding a child's custody.

Michael R. Turner, "Protecting Child Custody Rights for Service Members Should Be a Priority," in MikeTurner.com, February 28, 2010.

As you read, consider the following questions:

1. According to Turner, what situations do single mothers often confront upon their return from deployment?

2. Under what circumstances does Turner say the custody rights of service members first came to his attention?

3. What provision does the proposed bill make for the return of the service member from active deployment?

The stories are too frequent: a service member, many times a single mom, is called to serve her country and is given a short time to wind down her personal business and deploy. She makes temporary custody arrangements for her children usually with her former spouse, sometimes in the form of a non-binding family care plan. The mom is then deployed. Upon return from deployment, she goes to pick up her child, and finds out that her ex-spouse won't relinquish custody without a court order.

Legislation Should Protect Service Members in Child Custody Disputes

Sometimes the story is even worse. For example, a service member in fighting for custody in court has [his or her] custodial rights terminated by a judge simply because of "deployment" or even the "possibility of deployment." Deployed parents, serving our country in places like Afghanistan or Iraq, need protections from state courts disrupting these established family arrangements. We cannot have one branch of government asking American men and women to serve, while another branch punishes them for their service.

Over the past four years, I have introduced legislation to strengthen child custody protections so mothers and fathers in uniform will not be forced to lose custody of their children due to their military service. The purpose of this legislation is

My Child or My Country?

I was recently drawn to a photograph in a newspaper of a teary-eyed American soldier holding on to her child as if for dear life. The accompanying article told the story of a soldier, returning early from her deployment in Iraq, preparing to wage a "custody battle" stateside with her child's civilian father.

Before deployment, the soldier had done everything she thought necessary to protect her rights. She had obtained an order granting her primary physical custody, she had completed a family care plan, and she had arranged for temporary placement of the child with her mother during her deployment. What she had not anticipated was the civilian father waiting until her deployment to petition the court to modify the custody order, citing a "substantial change in circumstances." She wondered how this could happen when her child's father had rarely even exercised the visitation rights he already had.

This soldier's predicament is not unique.

Nakia C. Davis,
"Child Custody and the SCRA: My Child or My Country?"
Human Rights, *Spring 2008.*

straightforward: to protect our men and women in uniform from their deployment being used against them in child custody disputes.

This issue first came to my attention after Kentucky National Guard member Lt. Eva Slusher, who was deployed to serve her country, subsequently lost custody of her daughter, Sara. After a two-year, $25,000 court battle, Lt. Slusher was ultimately successful in regaining custody of her daughter but at a great financial and emotional cost.

Upon returning from deployment to Afghanistan, Lt. Col. Vanessa Benson of the 101st Airborne Division found herself in a year-long battle with her ex-husband to regain custody of her 14-year-old son, totaling more than $22,000 in legal fees. In December 2009, a Florida judge awarded her temporary custody. However, her legal fight continues to regain full custody.

"We're asked to drop everything to go to combat," Lt Col. Benson said in a December [2009] interview with CBS News. "Is it too much to ask that we have protection for when we come back to get our children back?"

This year [2010], I have introduced H.R. 4469 to amend the Servicemembers Civil Relief Act. The bill will protect the custody arrangements of service members during their deployment as well as prohibit the use of deployment as a factor in determining the best interests of a child in custody cases.

Furthermore, upon the return of the service member from deployment, any temporary change in custody would be immediately reversed, unless the reinstatement of custody is not in the best interest of the child. Finally, the amendment would not allow courts to consider a military parent's deployment or possible deployment as a basis for determining the best interests of the child in custody court cases.

Our men and women in uniform need this basic protection to provide them the peace of mind that the courts will not undertake judicial proceedings concerning their established custody rights while they are serving valiantly in contingency operations. Even a single incidence is one too many. This legislation seeks to protect them and their children.

> "[Congressman Michael R. Turner's bill]
> would have been [an] unwarranted in-
> trusion into domestic relations in the
> federal statutes, involving federal judges
> in a myriad of lawsuits for which they
> have little experience and even less abil-
> ity."

It Is Inappropriate for the Federal Government to Intervene in Custody Lawsuits Involving Military Personnel

Mark E. Sullivan

*Mark E. Sullivan practices family law in Raleigh, North Caro-
lina. He is the author of* The Military Divorce Handbook: A
Practical Guide to Representing Military Personnel and Their
Families, *published by the American Bar Association.*

*Although the bill Congressman Michael R. Turner intro-
duced to protect service members from loss of child custody during or following military deployment was well meaning, he chose
the wrong legislative body. According to Sullivan, the author of*

Mark E. Sullivan, "Urging Congress to Oppose Legislation That Would Create a Federal
Law of Child Custody Controlling State Custody Cases Involving Military Service Member Parents," *American Journal of Family Law*, vol. 23, Winter 2010, pp. 232–38. Copyright © 2010 Aspen Publishers, Inc. Reproduced by permission of Aspen Publishers.

this viewpoint, child custody disputes are clearly the province of state courts, and it is inappropriate to direct them to federal courts, where judges typically have scant experience in family law.

As you read, consider the following questions:

1. What were the four provisions of the bill introduced by Congressman Turner?

2. According to Sullivan, what are the two major reasons why military personnel lose custody of their children when they return from deployment?

3. What was the recommendation of the American Bar Association regarding a federal law to protect the custody rights of military personnel?

Seeking to insulate servicemembers from the loss of custody upon return from a deployment, Ohio Congressman Michael Turner introduced a bill in the 110th Congress which would have provided some protections for military custodians. Unfortunately, he chose the wrong legislature to consider the bill. The Ohio legislature, where the bill should have been filed, had passed a law stating that a parent's military service may be considered by the judge in deciding who receives custody. Instead, Rep. Turner introduced [legislation] as an attempt to amend federal law (the Servicemembers Civil Relief Act [SCRA], to be specific) to state that:

- Courts must restore custody of children to servicemembers (SMs) upon their return from deployment;

- The only exception would be where it could be shown by clear and convincing evidence that this was not in the child's best interest;

- The courts would not be able to consider an SM's absence upon deployment as a factor in determining the child's best interest;

- The courts would have been barred from changing child custody while an SM was deployed from the custody arrangement that existed at the time of deployment; and

- The only exception to this prohibition was if there was clear and convincing evidence that the change was in the child's best interest.

Family Law Is Not a Federal Matter

There is no question that disparate treatment of parents due to military service alone is generally inappropriate. In fact, the primary purpose of the Servicemembers Civil Relief Act ... is to eliminate the harsh consequences, penalties and adverse actions arising out of civil obligations—contract, lawsuits, taxes—for servicemembers who are unable to focus on military duties because of such issues. The act provides generously for stays of proceedings, appointment of counsel for the absent servicemember, prohibitions on default judgments, and authority for re-opening adverse judgments and orders.

However, the bill [which made it through the House and was only killed at the eleventh hour in the Senate] would have been [an] unwarranted intrusion into domestic relations in the federal statutes, involving federal judges in a myriad of lawsuits for which they have little experience and even less ability. It would have attacked a problem which does not exist to any reported extent, namely, the removal of custody from a servicemember due to deployment.

Again and again, case law shows that it is not the existence of military duties and resulting absences which cause problems for military members. There are no reported decisions involving the loss of custody by a military parent due to his or her deployment. Rather, the nature of the problem stems from two sources:

- The first is misuse of the courts and the SCRA by liti-
gants, parties who attempt to avoid the transfer of custody to the other parent (mandated by the "natural
parent presumption" when the other parent is not unfit
by reason of abuse, abandonment or neglect). These
military parents try to smuggle the child into the arms
of a relative (usually a stepparent or grandparent),
thereafter hiding behind the act in an attempt to stay
the court's hearing of the case upon the request of the
other parent for custody during the deployment.

- The second is the absence of informed counsel-lawyers
who understand both the SCRA and family law. When
the attorney for a military member doesn't know how
to request a stay of proceedings under [the SCRA], for
example, it is difficult to criticize a court which does
not side with the servicemember. Soldiers, sailors, ma-
rines and airmen have a right to expect competent and
qualified representation when their cases are pending
before the court. In some cases, they're not getting it.

There, then, are truly the primary causes of the problems
which servicemembers are facing upon return from deployment. Better training of the lawyers, better understanding of
the SCRA and conduct by servicemembers not new federal
custody laws—can remedy what problems exist.

In order to make clear to the House and Senate the opposition of America's largest group of lawyers to intrusions of
the federal government into the realm of family law, a traditional province for the state judiciary, the American Bar Association took up Resolution 106 at its midyear meeting in February 2009 and passed it. . . .

Recommendation of the American Bar Association

The recommendation calls for the American Bar Association
to urge Congress to oppose legislation that would create a fed-

eral law of child custody controlling state custody cases involving servicemember-parents. The recommendation urges that the legislation be stopped because it would dictate court outcomes in child custody cases, even where the child's best interests do not support that outcome; create federal-question jurisdiction over child custody cases, long the province of state courts; impose federally mandated evidentiary burdens on state courts; co-opt the growing body of state laws that comprehensively and appropriately address domestic relations matters affecting servicemembers; and cast doubt on existing servicemember protections found in the Servicemembers Civil Relief Act (SCRA). . . .

The issue arises from strong concern among child advocates, military legal assistance experts and others that the opposed legislation would inappropriately employ federal fiat to invade the province of the states by dictating court outcomes in child custody cases affecting deployed servicemembers. The opposed legislation provides that deployed servicemembers who had child custody at the time of their deployment would automatically have that custody restored upon their return, irrespective of other considerations affecting the best interests of the child. The opposed legislation would provide that custody could be denied to the returning servicemember in such a case only by a showing of "clear and convincing" evidence that it was not in the child's best interests. The opposed legislation improperly creates federal substantive law and evidentiary rules for custody determinations historically left to state courts. The opposed legislation would misuse the Servicemembers Civil Relief Act, the source of important procedural protections for servicemembers in litigation, to dictate substantive outcomes in custody cases. The legislation would cast doubt of the ample and adequate servicemember protections already found in the SCRA. The opposed legislation would create federal-question jurisdiction over these child custody cases, a role federal courts are ill equipped to fulfill. The opposed legislation would preempt the emerging body of state laws that comprehensively and organically address service-member domestic relations interests. The essence of the issue is that the opposed legislation is not in the interest of children or servicemembers.

The proposed policy would influence the United States Senate and the House of Representatives to oppose the legislation and thereby remove the threat to the interests of children and servicemembers posed thereby.

> *"There is no objective justification for brushing off the mothers as a bunch of prairie-style Stepford wives, let alone for leaping to the conclusion that mounting an armed raid to take their children away was indeed proper to do on the strength of a metaphor grounded in a religious stereotype."*

Religious Stereotypes Should Not Be Used to Take Children from Their Parents

Mary Zeiss Stange

Mary Zeiss Stange is a professor of women's studies and religion at Skidmore College and a member of USA Today's *board of contributors.*

The decision by the Texas Child Protective Services to remove more than four hundred children from a fundamentalist Mormon compound in Eldorado, Texas, based on allegations of underage marriage and sexual abuse, triggered the largest custody battle in U.S. history. This raid was precipitated by negative

Mary Zeiss Stange, "What Does Texas Church Raid Say About Us?" *USA Today*, May 12, 2008, p. 11A. Copyright © 2008, USA Today. Reproduced by permission of the author.

stereotypes of fundamentalist Mormons and their practice of polygamy and not by a careful weighing of evidence, according to Stange.

As you read, consider the following questions:

1. What other Texas case involving polygamy does the author say this case resembles?

2. What alternative explanation does Stange give for Eldorado mayor John Nikolauk's depiction of the women as "zombies"?

3. According to the author, when is it admissible to invoke the First Amendment to protect religious rights, and when is it inadmissible?

Before one applauds the roundup at the "FLDS [Fundamentalist Latter Day Saints] Corral," we should first look at what's taking place in the nation outside the Eldorado [Texas] compound—where anticult stereotypes can cause government to forget about some religions' pesky First Amendment protections.

The dust is more or less settling around the largest child custody case in Texas history. DNA samples and fingerprints having duly been taken, the 463 children removed by Texas Child Protective Services (CPS) from Warren Jeffs's Yearning for Zion (YFZ) Ranch, near Eldorado, have been trundled off to foster care throughout the state. A few nursing mothers are in group-home situations with their infants. The rest of the mothers, for whom supervised visitation with their children is being arranged by CPS, await custody hearings to be held by early June [2008].

Any charges of sexual abuse that ultimately emerge from the ongoing investigation will, of course, deserve the most vigorous prosecution. Meanwhile, the case raises some thorny questions, both about how we as a society regard religious "others," and about the role anticult stereotypes play in public decision making. These questions center on the treatment of those mothers and children.

Legal experts are divided on the legitimacy of what Barbara Walther, the presiding judge in the case, off-handedly referred to as the "cattle call" that removed those mothers and children from their home on April 3 [2008]. The closed federal warrant authorizing the raid relied heavily on phone calls, subsequently alleged to be a hoax, from 16-year-old "Sarah." Flora Jessop, formerly a member of a Fundamentalist Latter Day Saints (FLDS) community in Utah and now an anti-polygamy activist in Phoenix, had told Texas law enforcement that she had received similar calls from a "Sarah." Arguably, the raid was spurred more by negative stereotypes about FLDS and members' practice of polygamy than by a thorough investigation of evidence.

The Mt. Carmel Parallel

It isn't the first time this has happened to a religious group in Texas that diverged from the norm on the issue of plural marriage. The YFZ Ranch raid resembled, in some respects, what happened 15 years ago to David Koresh's Branch Davidians in Waco. Then, as in the FLDS situation, alarmed and alarming reports from disaffected former sect members fueled media "exposes" which, in turn, whipped up popular antagonism.

In 1992, CPS had investigated Mt. Carmel [Center, the name of the home of the Branch Davidians] and found no indications of child abuse. Yet the following year, after a 51-day standoff, then attorney general Janet Reno authorized the "dynamic entry" and use of tear gas against the Davidians out of concern, she said, for the children's welfare. The outcome was lethal: 80 Davidians, including Koresh, died in the resulting conflagration on April 19, 1993. When women didn't escape with their children, the FBI blamed the children's deaths on their mothers' failed "maternal instinct."

Rights Were Violated

It is easy to get caught up in the media hype regarding the alleged practices of this religious sect, and thus consider the removal of their children necessary or justified. However, our Constitution guarantees freedom of religion and the right to direct the upbringing of one's children without government interference, in absence of criminal action. All parents are entitled to due process prior to having their children taken, and this was not provided by either the agency or the court. If the state can take children without due process from this religious group, then it can take them from anyone whose religious or personal beliefs are disfavored by the state.

Gregory A. Hession, "Whose Children Are They, Anyway?"
New American, *June 22, 2008.*

A similar dynamic was at work in the raid on YFZ Ranch, although it was, as a spokesperson for the Texas Public Safety Department phrased it, more "diplomatic" than at Waco. "Not a shot was fired."

Appealing to anticult stereotypes, *Time* magazine quoted Eldorado Mayor John Nikolauk's description of the women being herded off the so-called compound looking like "zombies, with no expression in their eyes." This description doesn't square with what we subsequently saw of these women on the evening news. Perhaps their glazed expressions had something to do with being rounded up at gunpoint by SWAT teams, backed up by an armored personnel carrier and K9 dog units.

According to Marci Hamilton of the Cardozo Law School, the raid was justified because "there is nothing in the First Amendment that says that any religious group has the right to exist, no matter what they do."

This is true enough. Criminal prosecution is certainly appropriate when, in the name of religion, a clear violation of the law has occurred—as happened in Jeffs's conviction for facilitating the rape of a minor last year. (Koresh was likely guilty of statutory rape. We will never know for sure.) But the First Amendment does not sanction government repression of religious activities about which no clear harm has yet been proven—quite the contrary, in fact.

The FLDS women maintain that no child abuse occurred, that their relationships are spiritual and modeled on being "clean and pure," that they were at YFZ Ranch by choice. All of this is in line with FLDS's theological claim that it is merely adhering to the original Mormon tenets over which the sect split from the larger church (Latter Day Saints/LDS), when it abandoned polygamy somewhat over a century ago.

However, once again the authorities seem to suspect a failure of maternal instinct. A "tip sheet" issued to CPS workers dealing with the case—one source for which is Carolyn Jessop, who is hawking a book about her "escape" from FLDS—warns, among other things, that FLDS mothers may exhibit "learned and enforced helplessness," and a limited cultural mentality. As to the apparent hoax that spurred the raid, CPS spokeswoman Marleigh Meisner says that once authorities were convinced that abuse had occurred, the phone caller's actual existence became immaterial. "Sarah," Meisner explains, is a metaphor for young women subjected to abuse in the compound. "What we did," Meisner told CNN, "was warranted and in the best interest of the children. This is not about religion—this is about keeping children safe from abuse."

A flurry of press releases from CPS notwithstanding, the precise extent of the alleged abuse nonetheless remains unclear.

What Gives Me Pause

What is clear, however, is that there is no objective justification for brushing off the mothers as a bunch of prairie-style

Stepford wives, let alone for leaping to the conclusion that mounting an armed raid to take their children away was indeed proper to do on the strength of a metaphor grounded in a religious stereotype.

The feminist in me cringes at rising to the defense of a group so patently patriarchal as FLDS. But it isn't much of a stretch to defend the religious rights of groups with whom one mostly agrees, is it? I, personally, find the kind of spirituality practiced on the YFZ Ranch deeply troubling. I find the pop-romanticization of polygamy in HBO's *Big Love* equally problematic.

But, both as a feminist and as a scholar of religion, I also recognize that we as a society can applaud the YFZ raid and its potentially dire consequences for hundreds of women and their children, only if we blind ourselves to some other salient facts:

- Across the USA and across class, race, ethnic and religious divides, adolescent girls are becoming more sexually active, at ever-earlier ages. A recently released government study found that one in four teenage girls in this country has a sexually transmitted infection.

- Monogamy may be our societal "ideal," but given the American divorce rate, "serial polygamy" is closer to the norm—often culminating in precisely the pattern practiced by FLDS, whereby the older a man gets, the younger his newest wife is, the pattern originally advocated by Joseph Smith [the founder of the Latter Day Saints movement].

- Historians acknowledge a pragmatic link between the revelation that led the Mormon Church to renounce polygamy, and Utah statehood. On this ground, in religious terms, FLDS members are as legitimate in claiming to be "true" followers of Joseph Smith as are, say, those traditionalist Catholics who reject the authority of the post–Vatican II Roman Catholic Church.

- Gay marriage advocates have long pointed to parallels between anti-gay marriage and anti-polygamy laws: Both offer privileges to heterosexual monogamy.

- Meanwhile, polygamy and/or adolescent sexual intercourse are socially and religiously sanctioned in a variety of cultural contexts around the world, for example, in some Islamic communities, among the Maasai of Africa and in Papua New Guinea.

Maybe, rather than focusing on the family arrangements of an isolated Texas religious sect, we should be asking ourselves what was wrong with this picture: Even as CPS was herding the last of the FLDS girls off to distant foster care facilities late last month, American Internet users were so eager to see Annie Leibovitz's revealing *Vanity Fair* photos of 15-year-old Miley Cyrus that the magazine's website crashed.

> *"As more of the evidence is unveiled, the question will undoubtedly arise, Who thought it was safe to return these kids to the [Fundamentalist Latter Day Saints], and why?"*

If a Religious Group Abuses Children, the Children Should Be Protected

Katy Vine

Katy Vine is a reporter for Texas Monthly.

In a controversial custody case, more than four hundred children were removed from a Fundamentalist Latter Day Saints (FLDS) compound in Texas, based on charges of underage marriage and child abuse. Following an investigation that revealed the call charging child abuse was a hoax, Texas courts directed that the children be returned to the ranch and their parents. In the following viewpoint, Vine argues that this decision was ill considered, as further investigation revealed alarming stories about the treatment of women and girls on the compound.

Katy Vine, "With God on Their Side," *Texas Monthly*, October 2009, pp. 134–37, 218–25. Copyright 2009 Texas Monthly, Inc. Reproduced by permission.

As you read, consider the following questions:

1. What were some of the findings about the FLDS ranch that family law expert Charles Childress found alarming?

2. What action did Childress recommend, and what was the reason why this wasn't followed?

3. At the conclusion of the investigation, how many girls did the Texas Department of Family and Protective Services say had been victims of sexual abuse?

The conflict between the state of Texas and the FLDS [Fundamentalist Latter Day Saints] has played out on the battleground between government and religion, state and family. Familiar legal arguments, technicalities, and political postures and platitudes were standard components of the story line. Only now [2009], a year and a half after the raid, with all the children out of state custody and the trials of the twelve men set to begin, will the spotlight return to the crimes allegedly committed on the YFZ [Yearning for Zion] Ranch. And as more of the evidence is unveiled, the question will undoubtedly arise, Who thought it was safe to return these kids to the FLDS, and why? . . .

An Accusation of Abuse Began the Investigation

[In March 2008] an employee at a domestic abuse hotline in San Angelo, which is forty miles north of Eldorado, received a telephone call. The caller identified herself only as Sarah. She whispered into the phone so softly the worker could barely hear her. Sarah was hesitant to give any information. She'd pause for such long periods of time that the staffer had to ask if she was still on the line. The girl hung up and called back several times. With some patient prodding, Sarah revealed that she was sixteen years old, had an eight-month-old baby, was married, and lived at the YFZ Ranch, where her husband abused her. The hotline staffer wrote her report, and it was passed along to the office of Schleicher County sheriff David Doran.

Angie Voss, a supervisor for investigations at Child Protective Services [CPS], arrived at the ranch entrance after sunset, around nine, with nine caseworkers. . . . Jessop said that while there was no one at the ranch fitting the description of a sixteen-year-old named Sarah Barlow, he would allow the CPS team to interview girls at the schoolhouse.

Voss and her caseworkers began talking to the girls, one group at a time, but almost immediately she noticed a pattern of deception. "I was finding that the girls would switch their names," she would later testify. "They would use a different last name than they had previously reported, [or] wouldn't give a full name." Caseworkers seemed to be getting a lead on girls who fit the description of Sarah. But when the second group of girls was interviewed, Voss said, the conspiracy seemed to build: Suddenly not one of the girls knew her own date of birth. And there were signs that evidence was being destroyed. When Voss walked into a lower level of the schoolhouse, she saw a large shredder with the light still glowing red. Slices of paper were dangling from the machine, and two big bags nearby were stuffed with tattered documents.

By three in the morning, Voss realized she was in a bad situation. Her caseworkers had interviewed about 25 girls, and while they still hadn't found Sarah, they were beginning to discover what seemed to be a systematic practice of underage marriages. They were obliged to follow through on this information, but doing so was no easy task. "Some were forthcoming with information, some weren't," Voss testified. "They switch kids. They deny their children. I've encountered a few young girls that initially said they didn't have children at all, and then later reported they did." As the night wore on, she decided to remove 18 girls.

The investigation continued the next day, and by Friday night, she had grown fearful of the mounting tensions between the ranchmen and law enforcement. The previous night FLDS men had been standing in the schoolhouse stairwells, watching the caseworkers; some had video cameras. On Friday they climbed the trees to do countersurveillance with night-vision goggles. "I think what also added to my concern was that law enforcement had begun mobilizing a SWAT team, a tank, so you know, here I am trying to help children be safe in what felt like a very unsafe environment," she said.

Before long Voss decided to take all the children. Her position was that every child was indirectly related to these alleged victims of abuse and could not be interviewed properly at the ranch. "The little boys, the babies, the girls—what I have found is that they're living under an umbrella of belief that having children at a young age is a blessing, and therefore any child in that environment would not be safe," she testified. . . .

Over the next week, the children were removed from the ranch, and concerns escalated. Ultimately, the State of Texas removed 437 children; 139 women went voluntarily to be with their kids, leaving only 60 or 70 men and elderly women on the property. . . .

The Accusation Was Undermined by False Charges

The discovery of Sarah, meanwhile, was hardly a triumphant moment for the DFPS [Department of Family and Protective Services]. A Texas Ranger finally tracked her down in Colorado, only to find that she was not an FLDS member at all. Her real name was Rozita Swinton. She was a 35-year-old woman known for making false reports to police and women's shelters around the country. Investigators searched her apartment and found research notes about the FLDS. Dale Barlow, who was a real person and a member of the sect, was not

Copyright © 2008 by Pat Bagely and CagleCartoons.com. All rights reserved.

married to her. Swinton was charged with false reporting to authorities, a class three misdemeanor.

Before the public could even finish its collective gasp at the prospect of 437 children being taken away from their families on the basis of a hoax, DFPS commissioner Carey Cockerell presented a shocking briefing to the Senate Health and Human Services Committee. In an apparent attempt to recover some credibility, he claimed that half the girls aged fourteen to seventeen were pregnant or had already had children. This turned out to be untrue. He also noted that a lot of the kids had broken bones, but it was quickly pointed out that the number was probably average for a group of that many kids in a rural environment. The situation was rapidly becoming a PR [public relations] nightmare for the DFPS. In mid-April, when the department began removing the mothers, the previously reclusive FLDS spotted an opportunity and opened the ranch to the news media to tell its side of the story. Newspapers all over the country ran photos of sobbing women who'd recently been torn away from their children.

On April 18 Judge [Barbara] Walther ruled that the children should remain in state custody, and the kids were moved out of temporary facilities and placed in homes all over the state. Over the next few weeks, the DFPS took a beating. "Here we are sixty days later, and they're still treating everyone like a bunch of abusers," one attorney connected to the case told the San Angelo *Standard-Times*. "This is about winning at all costs for them," said an FLDS attorney. "This is out of control." Willie Jessop told the paper that the YFZ Ranch members had ordered five hundred to six hundred voter registration cards and intended to "put people in office with integrity." . . .

On May 22, 2008, the FLDS had its first victory. The Third Court of Appeals ruled that Judge Walther had lacked adequate evidence in ordering hundreds of children to remain in custody and that she had abused her discretion. Some lawyers applauded the decision, but child law experts grumbled that it was terrible. . . .

Chastened, the DFPS released a statement saying it would work with the office of Attorney General Greg Abbott to determine the state's next steps. . . . After the department filed a writ of mandamus with the Texas Supreme Court, arguing that the Third Court had abused its discretion, a Supreme Court spokesman received word that the attorney general's office was considering filing a brief. But hours later, the spokesman was told that that was no longer the case. . . .

The DFPS was left isolated and ultimately unable to prevail. On May 29, 2008, the Texas Supreme Court ruled that the Third Court of Appeals had not abused its discretion. The children were going home. . . .

A Further Investigation Reveals Disturbing Evidence

Not long after the Supreme Court's ruling, a white-haired, soft-spoken family law expert named Charles Childress came to work for the DFPS. . . .

[As] Childress's investigators combed through the evidence and reported their findings, he became alarmed. The documents acquired from the raid offered a wealth of revealing information. In particular, there was something called the Father's Family Information Sheet: Bishop's Record, which amounted to a Rosetta Stone to the family structures at the YFZ Ranch. Filled out in 2007, these self-reporting census pages identified the father of each family, along with his wives, his children, and their ages and residences. Childress quickly recognized a set of unsettling facts: Thirty-seven men living at the ranch one year earlier had 132 wives and 332 children. (These numbers reflect the records that have been released publicly; actual numbers may be higher. If there is a sheet on Warren Jeffs [president of the FLDS Church at the time of the raid], for example, that has been withheld.)

Other evidence raised more questions. There was the disparity in the ratio of teenage girls to teenage boys, for example. No one could explain why, in the twelve-to-seventeen-year age group, there were almost twice as many girls as boys. And then there was the white bed. Investigators' photographs taken in the YFZ Ranch temple show an adult-size bed with railings that appear to fold up like a crib's. On the bed's rumpled linens, investigators said they had found a long hair. A document that Childress had not seen but was obtained by *Texas Monthly* appears to be instructions for the construction of a similar bed. It describes a bed "covered with a sheet, but it will have a plastic cover to protect the mattress from what will happen on it." It also described "padded sides that can be pulled up that will hold me in place as the Lord does His work with me." What in the world was going on here?

Childress commuted every Monday to the DFPS office in San Angelo, spent the week there, and then returned to his home in Austin. He scoured the documents and reports late into the night, looking for the clearest possible picture of the FLDS lifestyle. Interviews that had been conducted with the mothers and children were far from reassuring. Girls told caseworkers there was no age requirement for a celestial marriage. When a Child Protective Services caseworker told Merrianne Jessop [a fifteen-year-old girl from the ranch] that if a thirteen-year-old girl was impregnated by a forty-year-old man it was considered sexual abuse—even if the two were spiritually married—Merrianne looked disgusted. She insisted that the marriages were "pure."

The investigators' stories contained similar accounts of women who were baffled by the scrutiny. One of Warren Jeffs's wives didn't see why caseworkers were concerned about her daughter, who had been married to a 34-year-old man a day after she'd turned fifteen. The mother told a representative of the Court Appointed Special Advocates (CASA) program that she didn't consider her daughter a victim and did not understand why her daughter couldn't visit with her new husband. After all, said the mother, she liked her new son-in-law.

Not every interview was as candid. Witnesses to the interviews say that some members seemed to be controlling the others. When one girl who said she had a ten-month-old child was asked her age, she looked at her husband, who told her, "You are eighteen." The girl then informed the investigator that she was eighteen. Texas state representative Drew Darby, of San Angelo, told me, "I saw what apparently was a nine-year-old boy and his mother talking to a CPS worker. The boy took his fist and hit his mom in the stomach, then made the motion of twisting his mouth with his hand as if he were locking his mouth with a key. I saw that." When a CASA representative visited the house of one woman, her daughter videotaped the meeting—but not to keep tabs on the interviewer. After the mother asked the CASA representative if they could speak outside, the girl followed them with the camera, saying she would leave them alone "only if she [her mother] will remember what not to talk about."

Childress urged action. A methodical man, he zeroed in on the department's pleadings. The official state forms, which Childress himself had designed when he worked for CPS in 1997, typically present a range of possible outcomes. The department begins by asking for temporary custody while the investigation is being conducted. Depending on the conclusions of the investigation, the DFPS may recommend reunification with the parents, which is always the first choice, or, in more serious cases, placement with relatives or other suitable adults. In the most serious cases, the DFPS can call for termination of parental rights so that the child can be adopted. "That is just standard pleading," Childress told me.

But in the FLDS cases, the state didn't follow the usual procedure. For some reason, the department chose not to include the possibility of terminating parental rights, meaning that any child that the DFPS thought was in danger would not be eligible for adoption but instead placed in foster care till age eighteen. Childress thought this strategy had tied the department's hands, because, even in the serious cases, it was difficult to argue that "it was in the best interest of the kids to be in foster care until they age out," he says. He wanted adoption on the table for the most egregious cases, but he was not in a position to change the pleadings without approval. Approval never came, and no one within the DFPS would tell him why.

Childress wasn't terribly impressed with the state leadership's understanding of the situation. "Going up to the governor, none of them had any idea what was going on," he says. . . .

As the months wore on, Childress went down to Austin to attend several meetings and explain his approach. One meeting included Albert Hawkins, the Health and Human Services commissioner; one included representatives from the attorney general's and governor's offices. Childress said he wanted to take some cases to trial. "They'd ask, 'Well, can you guarantee us it will win?' 'No, there's no such thing as a guarantee in a jury trial,' I said, 'but I'm pretty doggone certain that a West Texas jury hearing what all these people have been doing the last ten years is gonna be real reluctant to send these kids back to be raised by Warren Jeffs,'" Childress says. "I didn't get any feedback. . . . I think they just frankly lacked the courage."

And so, on October 23, Childress quit. . . .

The Result—A Lose-Lose Arrangement

This past summer, Commissioner [Anne] Heiligenstein told me that if allegations of abuse resurfaced at the YFZ Ranch, she wouldn't hesitate to intervene, though she believed such a scenario was unlikely. In her opinion, the FLDS had learned from this ordeal that Texas was intolerant of underage marriages. "It is our belief that future abuse to these and other children will no longer occur," she said. "The FLDS has too much to risk and too much to lose if they don't abide by the laws of Texas." In the end, the DFPS said that it had identified twelve girls, ranging from age twelve to fifteen, at the YFZ Ranch who had been victims of sexual abuse with the knowledge of their parents. Seven reached adulthood by the end of 2008, and three more have since reached adulthood. Two were twelve when they were married, three were thirteen, two were fourteen, and five were fifteen. Seven of those girls had one or more children. All were nonsuited with the exception of Merrianne Jessop, who was sent to live off the ranch with her new guardian, Naomi Carlisle.

If the plan all along has been to take aim at the problem of bigamy and underage marriage within the FLDS from a criminal angle instead of through civil proceedings, one can only imagine that the attorney general is holding his breath as the criminal trials get under way. (Perhaps he is also counting on additional convictions from an ongoing federal investigation regarding violations of the Mann Act and the Racketeer Influenced and Corrupt Organizations Act.) Jeffs is one of the twelve men who will be tried in Texas, though his court date has not yet been scheduled. But even if the state convicts all twelve and puts them in prison, nothing can stop Jeffs from continuing to direct his members with total disregard for the law.

"This is just a lose-lose deal," said a child psychiatrist who testified before the court. No clear pathway was without potentially devastating results. Charles Childress acknowledged that adoption was a traumatic option. But was it better, he asked, to return girls to families in which underage marriages had occurred and might occur again? "They think they're going to wind up happily holding hands in heaven," he said. "That doesn't make it something we can tolerate in a decent society."

"Although the idea of babies living the first months of their lives behind bars is sad to contemplate, many experts say that the alternative—separating them from their mothers—is far worse."

Young Children Fare Better Behind Bars with Their Incarcerated Mothers

Beth Schwartzapfel

Beth Schwartzapfel is a journalist based in Brooklyn, New York, and is an adjunct lecturer in the English department at La-Guardia Community College.

As of 2007, approximately four thousand women were pregnant when they entered prison, representing 4 percent of female inmates in state custody and 3 percent in federal prison, explains Schwartzapfel in the following viewpoint. In almost every case, the babies are taken from their mothers after birth. However, Schwartzapfel states, nine prisons in the country allow pregnant inmates to retain their children while in custody. These programs are an innovative way to ensure that the important early bonding relationship between mother and child isn't damaged, asserts Schwartzapfel.

Beth Schwartzapfel, "Lullabies Behind Bars," *Ms.*, vol. 18, Fall 2008. Copyright © 2008 Ms. Magazine. Reprinted by permission of Ms. Magazine and the author.

As you read, consider the following questions:

1. What statistics does the author cite to support her contention that the number of children with mothers in prison is growing exponentially?

2. What typically happens to children when their mothers go to prison?

3. What are some of the features of the Bedford Hills program for mothers and their babies?

It's midday on a recent Tuesday, and Rachael Irwin, 27, scurries across the floor on her hands and knees, playing peeka-boo with her 10-month-old daughter, Gabriella. The baby's big blue eyes dance with delight. Like many children her age, Gabriella is in day care. Unlike most children her age, though, Gabriella is in prison. She and her mother are participating in the Bedford Hills (N.Y.) Correctional Facility's nursery program, one of only nine programs in the country that allow incarcerated women to keep their babies with them after they give birth.

A Growing Number of Mothers in Prison

Nationwide, nearly 2 million children have parents in prison. The number of those with incarcerated mothers, in particular, is growing exponentially: A recent report from the Bureau of Justice Statistics found that the number of minors with mothers in prison increased by more than 100 percent in the last 15 years.

"These children are sort of victims by default," says Paige Ransford, research assistant at the Center for Women in Politics and Public Policy at the University of Massachusetts (UMass) Boston, and coauthor of the recent report "Parenting from Prison." Most of the children go live with grandparents or other relatives; one in 10 is placed in foster care. About half are separated from their siblings. These children are prone to a whole host of social developmental difficulties, and are more likely than their peers to be in trouble with the law later in life.

In the case of women who enter the system as mothers-to-be, the usual excitement of pregnancy is replaced with a sense of dread. The choices that, on the outside, are understood to be a woman's right—such as where and how to give birth, and whether or not to breastfeed—are transferred from the woman to bureaucrats and officers at the state Department of Corrections (DOC).

Of the 115,308 women incarcerated in the U.S. as of 2007, some 4,000 women—4 percent of women in state custody and 3 percent in federal—were pregnant when they entered prison. In the vast majority of cases, babies are removed from their mothers immediately after birth and placed with relatives or in foster care. However, a small but growing number of states are recognizing that the mother-child bond formed in the first few months of life is crucial to the child's development, and that the bond need not be broken.

Some States Keep Newborns with Mothers

"We're definitely seeing more states grapple with what it means to send women to prison, some of whom are pregnant," says Sarah From, director of public policy and communications for the Women's Prison Association (WPA) and coauthor of the agency's forthcoming report on prison nurseries. Eight states now have some sort of program to house female offenders together with their newborns, the newest being Indiana. The West Virginia legislature recently passed a bill establishing a program in its correctional facility for women, which is slated to open in 2009.

These programs vary widely in the length of time babies are allowed to stay with their incarcerated mothers and in the services provided while they're in prison with them. South Dakota's program allows babies to stay for just 30 days—with the mother in her regular cell—while Washington State allows children to stay for up to three years with their mothers in a separate wing of the prison. The Washington facility offers a federal Early Head Start program for prenatal health and infant-toddler development, and partners with the nonprofit Prison Doula Project to provide doula services to the women during and after pregnancies.

Originally started way back in 1901 when the prison was a state reformatory, the Bedford Hills program is the oldest and largest in the country, with its own nursery wing and space for up to 29 mother-baby pairs. Women live with their babies in bright rooms stuffed with donated toys and clothes. During the day, while the women attend DOC-mandated drug counseling, anger management, vocational training and parenting classes, their children attend a day care staffed by inmates who have graduated from an intensive two-year Early Childhood Associate vocational training program.

The Program Promotes Mother-Child Bonding

Although the idea of babies living the first months of their lives behind bars is sad to contemplate, many experts say that the alternative—separating them from their mothers—is far worse. "If a woman is serving a short sentence and can look forward to a life with her child . . . so much research addresses the importance of that early bonding relationship," says Sylvia Mignon, associate professor and director of the graduate program in human services at UMass Boston and coauthor, with Ransford, of the "Parenting from Prison" report. "The reality is, an infant does not know that she is in prison. All she knows is that she's getting the warmth and love and attention of this wonderful being called mom." Among women serving sentences of more than a decade, however, there is no clear consensus on what's best for the child; the Bedford Hills program generally only accepts women serving sentences of five years or less. "We don't want to create a bond that's guaranteed to be broken," says the children's center program director, Bobby Blanchard.

Unlike in the general prison population, doors in the program are never locked; inmates must be able to come and go freely in order to warm bottles, do laundry and comfort crying children out of the earshot of other sleeping babies. Rooms are decorated with photographs and handmade posters that say things like, "Loving yourself is something to be proud of!" Danielizz Negron, 23, rocks her four-month-old son, Jeremiah, while he naps in a stroller. She was six months pregnant when, after a year of fighting burglary charges, she accepted a plea deal and turned herself in. "If I had not known about this program, I would not have came in. I would've been in Mexico somewhere by now," she says, only half joking.

As the number of prison nurseries continues to grow, some caution against becoming overly sanguine. Prison nurseries are wonderful programs, says the WPA's Sarah From, however "we shouldn't be looking to build more prison nurseries, but rather work in the community to put less women in prison."

> "Residents, including children . . . are
> kept in tiny cells, denied adequate
> medical care, forced to wear prison garb
> and exposed to potentially traumatiz-
> ing indignities."

Imprisoning the Children of Illegal Immigrants Is Traumatic for the Children

Ellis Cose

Ellis Cose is a contributing editor, columnist, and author for Newsweek *magazine. The T. Don Hutto Residential Center in Taylor, Texas, was a former prison that the Department of Homeland Security decided to use as a means to house undocumented families. American Civil Liberties Union staff attorney Vanita Gupta, along with immigration lawyer Barbara Hines, argues that the facility remains a prison. The residents—including children—are forced to live in tiny cells, wear prison clothing, and are denied sufficient medical care. These conditions expose children to an unnecessary trauma. The author claims that*

Ellis Cose, "American-Born, but Still 'Alien'? A Spate of Local Immigration Initiatives Expresses Concern About Leadership Failures on a Federal Level, and About Mounting Costs Borne by the States," *Newsweek*, March 19, 2007. Reproduced by permission.

the opening of this residential facility, along with a raid that re-sulted in the apprehension of undocumented workers, shows signs of the anxiety about illegal immigrants.

As you read, consider the following questions:

1. According to Leo Berman, what is a U.S. citizens "most precious benefit"?

2. Did the spokesman for Immigration and Customs En-forcement directly address the allegations against the T. Don Hutto center?

3. As stated in the viewpoint, what happened in New Bed-ford, Massachusetts?

When a pregnant woman "waits on the border," as Leo Berman puts it, for her chance to cross illegally to give birth in the United States, she is "committing a crime"—one for which neither she nor her child should be rewarded. Ber-man, a Texas state representative, feels so strongly about this that he is prepared to relegate U.S.-born children of undocu-mented immigrants to second-class status. "Our most precious benefit is U.S. citizenship," he said in his office in the capitol. "And U.S. citizens should be concerned if we are giving it away 350,000 times a year" to children born to undocumented mothers.

Berman, a Republican, has authored a bill that would com-pel Texas to deny benefits to children of what he calls "illegal aliens." He knows the bill, which flies in the face of legal pre-cedent, would face immediate challenge. "We want to go into federal court," Berman says. "The mail on this is running 50 to 1 in support." The courts, he believes, would agree with his contention that the 14th Amendment, mandating equal pro-tection, "does not apply to foreigners." Berman has another bill pending that would assess an 8 percent tax on money sent south of the border.

Berman, a retired Army lieutenant colonel, fears America is being overrun. And if the Feds won't act, he will. Berman may be extreme, but he's not alone. Across America, state officials and local politicians are insinuating themselves into the immigration debate. In the past several months, multiple cities have passed ordinances targeting undocumented immigrants. The measures, which make it a crime to employ or rent to those here illegally, have been contested in courts by organizations like the ACLU [American Civil Liberties Union] and the Puerto Rican Legal Defense and Education Fund, which argue that local officials have no role to play in formulating immigration policy.

T. Don Hutto Residential Center

Barbara Hines, an immigration lawyer and professor at the University of Texas, says the immigration issue has grown "louder, more exacerbated" in recent months. Vanita Gupta, a staff attorney with the ACLU, says there is "a whole new wave of fear and demonization." She points to the decision by the Department of Homeland Security last year [2006] to house undocumented families in a converted prison—the T. Don Hutto Residential Center [formerly known as the T. Don Hutto Family Residential Facility]—in Taylor, Texas.

Last week [in March 2007] Hines and Gupta sued over conditions at the facility. They contend that Hutto remains a prison in everything but name. Residents, including children, they say, are kept in tiny cells, denied adequate medical care, forced to wear prison garb and exposed to potentially traumatizing indignities. When she first visited the center, says Hines, "I was shocked. I had never seen children in a prison before."

A spokesman for Immigration and Customs Enforcement [ICE]—the enforcement arm of Homeland Security—read a statement to *Newsweek* describing Hutto as a modern facility "designed to humanely accommodate families and children," but would not directly address allegations in the lawsuit since

Special Challenges for Undocumented Mothers

An incarcerated mother with undocumented immigration status has almost no chance of avoiding termination of parental rights if sentenced to a lengthy prison term. The conspicuous lack of research and publications relating to incarcerated mothers with undocumented legal status—and the lack of literature about undocumented persons in general—is indicative of the lack of attention on this vulnerable population. Little is published at all about undocumented immigrants with the exception of conservative rhetoric about the economic costs of "illegal aliens." Undocumented immigrants are portrayed as criminals, depriving legal citizens of jobs and a burden on health, education, and welfare systems. In contrast, the media rarely provides images of undocumented immigrants as marginalized persons in need of protection. . . .

Children of undocumented immigrants may suffer the most as a result of punitive criminal justice and child welfare policies and practices. Many children of undocumented immigrants are U.S. citizens and are entitled to services and protection. Unfortunately, protection may not include a right to remain with one's own family or members of their cultural background.

Pamela Stowers Johansen,
"Incarcerated Mothers: Mental Health, Child Welfare Policy,
and the Special Concerns of Undocumented Mothers,"
California Journal of Health Promotion, *2005.*

the agency does not talk about pending litigation. Last week an ICE-led inquiry resulted in the apprehension of several people connected to a leather-processing plant in New Bedford, Mass., that allegedly hired scores of undocumented workers.

The opening of Hutto, the raid in New Bedford and the initiatives bubbling up from local officials are all signs of a level of anxiety about illegal immigration not seen in years. Behind the proposals from Berman and others is a real concern about the leadership failure at the federal level and about mounting costs borne by the states. At [Parkland] Hospital in Dallas, for example, a spokesperson said that some 75 percent of total deliveries there were paid for by a Medicaid benefit aimed at women who can't provide proof of citizenship. Royce West, a Texas state senator who is pro-immigrant, has put forth a bill, less onerous than Berman's, that would tax international money transfers. The proceeds would go toward indigent health care.

Immigration Bill

Last May the Senate passed an immigration bill authored by Ted Kennedy and John McCain, which the House rejected. Kennedy and McCain are likely to offer another bill, perhaps as early as this week, focusing on border enforcement, legalization and a new guest-worker program. Those ideas constitute a natural starting point for an intelligent national discussion on the issue. With Democrats in control of Congress and talk of reform in the air, the House may be more inclined to participate this time. If it doesn't, we may be doomed to see the arena dominated by some local politicians who think that doing something—even something that's probably unconstitutional—makes them better than the do-nothing Feds.

Periodical and Internet Sources Bibliography

The following articles have been selected to supplement the diverse views presented in this chapter.

Nakia C. Davis	"Child Custody and the SCRA: My Child or My Country?" *Human Rights*, vol. 35, no. 2, Spring 2008.
Lauren S. Douglass	"Avoiding Conflict at Home When There Is Conflict Abroad: Military Child Custody and Visitation," *Family Law Quarterly*, vol. 43, no. 2, Summer 2009.
Sarah Harper	"Illegal Immigrant Detained in Police Raid May Lose Custody of Son," LawyerShop.com, April 30, 2009. www.lawyershop.com.
Gregory A. Hession	"Whose Children Are They, Anyway?" *New American*, June 22, 2008.
Adam Kilgore and Peter Slevin	"400 Children Removed from Sect's Texas Ranch," *Washington Post*, April 8, 2008.
Phyllis Schlafly	"No Way to Treat Our Soldiers," Eagle Forum, September 7, 2005. www.eagleforum.org.
Jeffrey P. Sexton and Jonathan Brent	"Child Custody and Deployments: The States Step in to Fill the SCRA Gap," *Army Lawyer*, December 2008.
Ginger Thompson	"After Losing Freedom, Some Immigrants Face Loss of Custody of Their Children," *New York Times*, April 22, 2009.
Ann Scott Tyson	"Fighting War—and for Custody," *Washington Post*, December 30, 2008.
David Usborne	"'No Justification' for Raid on Texas Mormon Ranch," *Independent*, May 24, 2008.

OPPOSING
VIEWPOINTS®
SERIES

CHAPTER 4

Should Abduction Be Used in International Custody Disputes?

Chapter Preface

Richard Haddad and his girlfriend split in 2006 when their daughter was only two months old. Joint custody was established and the former couple worked out a schedule where their daughter was exchanged at a day care center every two weeks. Despite these arrangements, the custody was described as "high conflict," with allegations of domestic violence against Haddad. On October 6, 2008, when the mother went to pick up her daughter at day care for her two-week stint, the daughter wasn't there. She contacted Haddad, who asked that the daughter remain with him for a few additional days. However, when the child wasn't returned for a court hearing scheduled for October 22, the mother filed a report with the Henderson, Nevada, police department. An investigation revealed that Haddad had applied for and received a passport for the child on October 8 and that the father and daughter flew from Phoenix to Calgary, Canada, on October 14, 2008.

The child was missing for six weeks. Following a coordinated search involving the Henderson Police Department, the Federal Bureau of Investigation, the National Center for Missing and Exploited Children, and the Canadian Border Services Agency, among other agencies, the child was found at a Calgary day care center while Haddad was gambling in a Canadian casino. The daughter was reunited with her mother on December 8, 2008. In January 2009, Haddad was convicted on a felony charge of removing a child from the person having lawful custody, and he was given a prison term of between eighteen months and four years, plus a $5,000 fine. Unfortunately, not all international parental abduction stories are resolved so swiftly.

International child abduction, a dramatic response by parents in some contentious child custody cases, has increased dramatically in the past few years. In the twelve months from

October 1, 2008, to September 30, 2009, there were 1,135 cases representing 1,621 children reported to the United States Central Authority of children abducted from the United States to another country. These numbers represented almost twice the number of cases in the 2005 to 2006 report year. Additionally, during the 2008 to 2009 report year, 324 cases representing 454 children were reported of children abducted from a foreign country to the United States. During the 2008–2009 period, 436 children were returned to the United States, with 74 percent of these children being returned from a country that signed the Hague Convention on the Civil Aspects of International Child Abduction. The Hague Abduction Convention, a treaty signed by sixty-nine countries, seeks to protect children from the harmful effects of abduction and retention across international boundaries by providing a procedure to bring about their prompt return. Additionally, the Hague Abduction Convention generally honors the custody arrangements in place prior to the abduction, with the goal of preventing parents from abducting a child to a country where courts might be more favorable to their custody claims.

Why the dramatic increase in international child abductions? Experts point to several reasons. Among them are the ease of international travel, a growing number of bicultural marriages, and the fact that the United States requires the permission or presence of only one parent for a child to travel outside the country. The issues surrounding international parental child abduction are debated in the viewpoints in the following chapter.

> *"We cannot condone the violation of the law of another sovereign territory,' a State Department spokesperson says of private recovery attempts. . . . [Yet a State Department employee who e-mailed Todd Hopson said,] 'We all breathed a collective sigh of relief on hearing that Andres and Helen are back home in Florida with you.'"*

Sometimes Abduction Is the Only Way to Regain Custody

Nadya Labi

Nadya Labi is a writer based in New York City.

Despite the guidelines of the Hague Convention on the Civil Aspects of International Child Abduction, in 2009 more than three thousand children residing abroad had been abducted from the United States, according to U.S. State Department files. Most of these children were in countries that either were not signatories to the convention or had corrupt legal systems, according to Labi in the following viewpoint. In these instances, the most effective recourse for the "left-behind" parent may be to hire someone who will snatch back the child, she writes.

Nadya Labi, "The Snatchback," *Atlantic Monthly*, vol. 304, November 2009, pp. 76, 78, 80, 83–84, 86–89. Reproduced by permission of the author.

As you read, consider the following questions:

1. What are some of the reasons the author gives for the increased number of child abduction cases tracked by the U.S. State Department?

2. What is the other side of this story, from the perspective of Jason Alvarado, the biological father whose son was taken from him?

3. While not officially condoning the recovery of Andres from his biological father in Costa Rica, a State Department employee quoted in this viewpoint was supportive of it. What reasons did she give?

On a humid Thursday afternoon in February, I am riding in a rented van in Central America with a man who abducts children for a living. The van's windows are tinted, and Gustavo Zamora Jr. is speeding east on a two-lane highway toward Siquirres, a town buried in the lush abundance of eastern Costa Rica. Gus is planning to snatch Andres, a 9-year-old American boy who has been claimed by too many parents. Sitting behind me is one of them: Todd Hopson, a 48-year-old lawyer from Ocala, Florida, who considers himself the boy's father, by rights of love and U.S. law. Ahead of me in the front passenger seat is Gus's 22-year-old son and partner, Gustavo Zamora III.

"That's too far for a switch," the elder Zamora, 53, is saying, pointing to a hotel 10 miles outside of Siquirres. His plan is to use two vehicles for what he calls the "recovery," or "snatchback." Once he gets Andres, he intends to drive a white Toyota SUV [sport-utility vehicle] to a switch point, where he will abandon the SUV and put Andres in the van. That way, any witnesses to the snatchback will report seeing the SUV headed west in the direction of the capital, San José—while in fact Gus and Andres will be in the van headed southeast toward Panama. But this hotel won't work. "We definitely can't come all the way back down this way," Gus says. "I want to make time."

Todd Hopson's Complex Story

Even by the standards of this American age of divorce, when byzantine custody arrangements are commonplace, Andres's situation is complex. His biological mother, Helen Zapata, who is from Costa Rica but now lives in America, was married to Todd Hopson for just under three years. Now they are divorced—but they continue to share custody of Andres and, until recently, lived together in Florida. Todd never formally adopted Andres, but he and Helen got an official document in Florida in June of 2008 acknowledging Todd's legal paternity. They also asked a Florida court to declare Andres "born of their marriage," a request that was granted the following September and applied retroactively to 2004, the year they divorced.

"I got to thinking—what if something happens to me, and Andres has Helen's last name? Andres wouldn't be entitled to any rights or benefits," Todd told me. "I'm a lawyer and should have been thinking about those things earlier, but I didn't."

At the end of June 2008, Helen flew to Costa Rica to spend time there and, with Todd's support, to enroll in a drug clinic to kick a cocaine habit. Every year, Helen and Andres traveled to Costa Rica to visit not only Helen's relatives, but also those of Jason Alvarado, who is Andres's biological father. So that June, as usual, Andres went along, though he didn't want to go—he didn't want to miss Little League season in Ocala, for one thing. Before Helen left the U.S., she called Jason in Costa Rica, asking if he would look after Andres for a few days and saying that she planned to go job hunting in Costa Rica so that she could move there permanently. "I lied to him" to hide the drug problem, Helen concedes. When Jason learned Helen's true whereabouts, he called Todd in Florida, thanking him for everything he'd done for Andres and telling him, Todd says, that he planned to raise the boy himself.

Todd felt blindsided. He had thought Andres would be visiting with Helen's mother and told me he had "no idea that Jason had any interest" in having custody of Andres. As Todd saw it, Jason had never previously tried to gain custody or in any way contributed to Andres's care. "If you're going to be the father," Todd says, "you don't let someone else pay the freight."

Todd consulted with the U.S. Embassy in Costa Rica, which advised him to proceed with his plan to pick up Andres in early August. But when Todd flew to Costa Rica, Jason would not let him talk to the boy. Todd was livid. He had hoped to reason with Jason, but he realized that the man had no intention of backing down. So Todd got an injunction from a San José court ordering Jason to surrender Andres, and he and Helen accompanied the Costa Rican police when they went to Jason's office to deliver it. Jason still refused to relinquish Andres, and Todd says the police told him that they didn't have the right under Costa Rican law to enter Jason's home and take the boy. Todd returned to Florida while Helen stayed in Costa Rica. Later in August, Jason challenged Helen's maternal fitness in light of her drug habit and won temporary custody of Andres from a different Costa Rican court.

The Hague Convention on the Civil Aspects of International Child Abduction was drafted in 1980 to resolve custodial claims between what are known as the "taking parent" and the "left-behind parent." To date, 81 nations, including the United States, in 1988, have agreed to the treaty. The State Department, which enforces the treaty in the U.S., currently has more than 2,000 active cases involving nearly 3,000 children abducted from the U.S. or wrongfully retained abroad. In 2008, it opened 1,082 new files, an increase of more than 25 percent over 2007. (The increase reflects a rise in transnational marriages, and consequently transnational divorces, as well as growing awareness of the Hague Convention.)

Todd considered filing a Hague [Convention] application with the State Department, but he was skeptical that it would amount to anything because he distrusted what he dismissed as the corrupt legal system in Costa Rica. The application, he feared, could take months to process. He wavered between feelings of fury and utter helplessness. "It breaks my heart," he said to me. "I don't have any control." Determined to regain some, he surfed the Internet for security agencies in Costa Rica, thinking, "I'll hire some bodyguards and just take Andres." A man Todd spoke to at one agency said he didn't do child recoveries but could recommend someone who did: Gus Zamora. "That's all he does," the man said. . . .

Todd Contacts a Child Abduction Specialist

In late August, even before Todd filed a Hague [Convention] application, he contacted Gus Zamora, who was feeling the pinch of the recession. It had been nine months since his last recovery. "If somebody asked me to find his dog or cat on a roof, I'd do it," he joked. Gus offered to do the job for $25,000, including expenses—about a third of his usual rate. Still, Todd had to borrow money against his house to pay the fee. Gus planned to take two trips to do the recovery, and Todd agreed to pay him $10,000 before the first and $15,000 before the second.

In September, Gus flew from Tampa to Costa Rica to rendezvous with Helen and do reconnaissance in Siquirres. From the start, Helen resisted doing a recovery; she didn't want to break any laws and possibly jeopardize her ability to return to Costa Rica. Todd felt he needed her cooperation, however, because she had access to Andres—and Andres's passport had her last name on it. (A child traveling with adults without the same last name might raise suspicion.) At Todd's insistence, Helen agreed to meet with Gus. . . .

Plans for the "Snatchback"

"Don't drive fast, especially on the wet roads," Gus counsels Helen, who is standing under the awning of the purple motel, watching the rain pour down. It's 6 a.m. on Tuesday. The parrots are chirping, and the palm trees bend under the weight of the water. "Take your time and get here," Gus adds. "It's only a couple of minutes."

Gus is prepping Helen to snatch Andres at the bus stop. If a stranger like Gus tried to grab the boy, witnesses might intervene, and the police would react immediately. But a mother calling out to her son and inviting him to step into her car might not trigger an alarm. Ordinarily, Gus would ride along in the car with Helen, but he doesn't trust her. He also has doubts about whether Andres will go with his mother. He has more faith in Todd's relationship with the boy, so he has decided that Todd should be in the SUV with Helen. Gus and his son will wait in the getaway van at the purple motel, preparing for a run to the Panama border. . . .

At 7:00, a white bus stops on the town square. No one boards it. There are no schoolkids at the bus stop. "I don't see any activity." Todd says, sighing.

Time passes. The only rounds are the relentless pounding of the rain, the *swish* of the wipers, and Helen's occasional sniffs.

Suddenly, Helen sits bolt upright. "That's Jason. You see?" A blue Camry heads toward us and turns left onto the street perpendicular to ours. She warns Todd to duck down.

"So where's Andres?" Helen says, perplexed. Why didn't Jason pull over at the bus stop? Why did he turn onto the side street instead? Could Andres's bus stop be located on that side street—not by the square, as she had thought? She asks Todd whether she should check out the side street. He encourages her to go.

"I don't know if we should," she says, even as she turns the ignition, inching forward and looking from side to side. She turns right, following the route the blue car took.

"Oh, here," Helen gasps, looking at two boys in identical uniforms—dark-blue polo shirts and khaki pants—standing along the side of the road. She puts down the passenger-side window, shouting: "Come, Andres! Ven, Andres!"

The shorter and slimmer of the two boys, who has close-cropped hair and a light scar on his brow, stares at her. His brown eyes widen, and he steps forward slightly. Then he looks at the other boy, looks back at Helen, and shakes his head.

"He says no," Helen says. Putting up the window.

"Did Chino see me?" Todd asks, referring to Andres's companion, who is his uncle. Helen says yes. Todd tells Helen to get out of the car and get Andres.

"He doesn't want me to," she says.

"Go out and get him, Helen," Todd says, his voice rising in frustration. "Just go out and get him." Helen drives on. Todd moves aggressively into the space between the front seats, directing Helen to do a U-turn and return to Andres. She obeys, warning Todd that Andres's bus is coming.

"I don't care, because we're made. Let's go," Todd shouts. "I'm going to get him. Just go!" Helen sniffs, and Todd orders her to stop the SUV. He leaps out and goes to Andres, who is wearing an olive-green backpack.

"Let's go," he says, touching Andres's shoulder "Come on, buddy!"

Helen adds her encouragement from the driver's seat. "Come, Andres!"

Andres hesitates, glances at Chino, and then walks quickly to the open door of the SUV. Todd throws himself into the SUV behind Andres and slams the door. "Go!" he shouts.

Helen hits the accelerator.

"Hi, buddy," Todd says to Andres, hugging him. "How are you, sweetie?"

"Hi," Andres mutters. He's clearly unnerved.

"Don't worry, Papi," Todd assures him. "It's going to be okay."

In the rearview mirror, Helen can see Chino running toward the yellow house. Todd tells her to focus on the road. "Nice and easy," he says. But Helen careens around the corner, narrowly missing an old man on a bicycle as she swerves to avoid an oncoming bus. As she drives, she keeps asking Andres why he refused to come to her. "He's scared," Todd says.

Helen turns onto Highway 32, smack into a long line of traffic. Todd kisses Andres. "Who's following us?" Andres asks. Helen keeps glancing behind us, worried that Jason will be there. As the SUV creeps forward in the traffic, she pounds the heel of her right hand on the steering wheel, shouting at the cars. "They need to move!"

"It's okay, it's okay, buddy," Todd keeps saying to Andres, who sits rigidly, staring out of eyes that seem to have lost their ability to blink. "That car just happened to be behind us. I don't think they were following us."

The palm trees in front of the purple motel come into view, and Helen turns sharply to the right before veering left and screeching to a halt. Gus and his son are waiting in the van, eyebrows raised.

Helen, Todd, Andres, and I jump out of the SUV. Gustavo hustles us into the van.

"Let's go," Gus shouts from the driver's seat.

Helen remembers that she's left the keys in the SUV.

"Leave 'em," Gus barks. "Everybody duck down—you especially," looking at Helen. "Your big head has got to duck down. Don't worry about anything. Just stay down until we get a safe distance away."

Gus roars out of the parking lot and turns left onto the highway, heading east. A blue Camry speeds past us in the opposite direction. . . .

A "Shock and Awe" Rescue

The day after the snatchback in Siquirres, *Diario Extra*, a popular tabloid in Costa Rica, reports that while Andres was waiting for the bus, a white Toyota SUV stopped, and two women and a man "violently grabbed" him. The newspaper lists Helen, an aunt, and a U.S. national named "Hotson" as suspects. The article includes a photo of Andres and instructs anyone who spots him to call the police. Jason's wife is quoted: "We are confident, given that only a few hours have gone by, that they would not be able to take him out of the country."

But while the police search for Andres in a white Toyota SUV, we are speeding toward Panama in a beige Dodge Caravan. Andres and Helen lie against each other in the backseat, and Todd is prone against the side door. Gus is at the wheel.

"Andres looks good," Todd says. "That was some shock and awe."

After nearly an hour, Gus has fought his way through traffic to the turnoff to Limón. Except for some overhanging palm trees and piles of trash, the road is clear. At Gus's say-so, we sit up. Helen pulls off Andres's dark-blue shirt so he can exchange it for a white T-shirt that says Cornerstone Middle School.

"You want to go home, right?" Todd says.

Andres nods.

"You remember, I promised," Todd says. "Did you think Daddy wasn't going to come for you?"

Andres shakes his head.

Todd tells Andres that he's left his room exactly the same and that a package has arrived all the way from Japan for him—a customized baseball glove.

"Your hair looks great, buddy," Todd says, kissing him and observing that he's grown a little Mohawk. Gus's son informs Todd that the correct term is *faux-hawk*.

Andres takes care with his appearance; he is a handsome boy who looks like a miniature version of his favorite Yankee, A-Rod [Alex Rodriguez]. He tells Todd that he's started using a hair gel called Gorilla Snot. Later, he asks if he'll be able to buy the gel in Florida. Throughout the journey, Andres says little, but he seems most concerned about having "forgotten" things—like the hair gel, his clothing, his iPod charger, his Nintendo DS, and, most important, two of his baseball gloves. He had taken them with him to Costa Rica, even though he didn't play much baseball in Siquirres.

As "What's Love Got to Do with It?" plays on the radio in the background and the ocean crests by the side of the road, Todd tells Andres, "I was so angry when I came down and they wouldn't let me have you."

Andres says nothing. But he smiles a few minutes later when Todd cracks a joke about the snatchback, saying: "I was going to tell you, 'Come with me if you want to live.'"

Gus drives past dilapidated shacks with corrugated-iron roofs, huddles of thin brown cows, and fields of banana plants, their bunches of fruit cradled in bright-blue plastic bags. After an hour, we arrive at Sixaola, a town that shares a narrow river with Panama and lies in the shadow of a border crossing. Trucks idle on a graffiti-covered concrete overpass that runs through the town. Gus's plan is to get Todd and his family to Panama without passing through an official border stop. Presenting them to immigration officials in Costa Rica at this point is too risky.

Gus frets about finding his contact, a Nicaraguan who owns a motorboat in Sixaola. Luckily, "the Nica," as Gus calls him, is at his home—a rickety contraption consisting of sheets of iron on a wooden base. The Nicaraguan goes off to fetch the boat. While we wait, Gus reverses the van, rocking it back and forth on the edge of an embankment, which is littered with rotting banana peels and tin cans. Finally, he manages to squeeze the van next to a pigpen in the backyard of the man's home.

Andres gets out of the van. He plays with a purple band on his wrist and fingers his faux-hawk until a blue boat pulls up to the embankment. He steps into the rocking boat. The engine sputters to life. Minutes later, the captain hops onto Panamanian soil and ties the boat to a banana plant. Todd, Andres, and Helen walk across a stretch of swamp and step into a black pickup with tinted windows that Gus has arranged to have waiting for them.

Andres Adjusts Well

It's time for the Little League play-offs between the Red Sox and the Bulls at the Ocala Rotary Sportsplex. Andres—Hopson displayed on the back of his dark-blue shirt—stands on the first-base line next to his teammates, listening to "The Star-Spangled Banner" with his hat over his heart. The music stops, and Andres's coach shouts, "All right, gentlemen, let's go out there and throw some balls!" Soon, Andres is up at bat. He goes down in the count, two strikes against him. He stares through his mirrored sunglasses at the pitcher, a scrawny boy with a mean right arm, and swings at the next ball. The bat connects and he races to first, sliding in safe.

It's as if Andres never left Ocala. He wakes up every day at 7:10 a.m., takes a shower, and has a bowl of Lucky Charms. Then Todd drives him to the Cornerstone School, a private school with banners along its halls promoting mutual respect and appreciation—no put downs. Miss Candice, his third grade teacher, says she has observed no ill effects from his absence. He does his assignments on time, and he is the Four Square star of the playground. Todd's relationship with Helen broke down, however, not long after their return, and he asked her to move out.

Todd considered taking Andres to a psychologist, but he decided against it because the boy seemed fine. In response to my direct questions, Andres says that the Alvarados treated him well but that he doesn't miss anything about Costa Rica. He didn't play baseball in Siquirres. It's "funner" in Ocala, where he plays baseball three times a week. He says he knew his dad would come for him. Andres doesn't like to talk about Costa Rica. If anyone asks where he was, he told Todd upon his return, "I'm going to say it's a long story."

But as Jason Alvarado sees it, the story is simple. Helen Zapata and Todd Hopson kidnapped Andres. Andres, he says, had been adjusting well to Siquirres; he had even been president of his class. Jason says he doesn't want to appear ungrateful to Hopson for raising Andres. Still, he believes Andres's care should be a matter between him and the boy's mother. "Now that his mother seems not to be able to take care of him, I don't see why he has to stay" in the U.S., Jason says. "They have always known I'm the father. I have always been there for him emotionally and economically." Todd, for his part, says that Jason never spent "one centavo" on Andres's care; Jason counters that he sent money to Helen.

In theory, the U.S. State Department agrees with Jason's view. "We cannot condone the violation of the law of another sovereign territory," a State Department spokesperson says of private recovery attempts. Yet when Todd informed the State Department that he had, with Gus Zamora's help, recovered Andres, the woman helping with his Hague [Convention] application responded by e-mail, "We all breathed a collective sigh of relief on hearing that Andres and Helen are back home in Florida with you." She went on to explain that Costa Rica had "a steep learning curve" about the convention, and said of Hopson's application, "We frankly do not know how it might have worked in your case."

Jason is giving them another chance to find out: in late May, he filed his own Hague [Convention] application, requesting his son's prompt return.

"The particular advantage of mediation [is that] the procedure is not limited to the issues under legal dispute, but rather open to a much wider range of topics the participants need to settle."

Mediation Is Preferable to Abduction to Resolve Custody Disputes

Christoph C. Paul and Jamie Walker

Christoph C. Paul specializes in family law in the law firm Paul & Partner in Berlin, Germany. Jamie Walker is a mediator and mediation trainer with the Bundesverband Mediation e.V. (Federal Mediation Association).

Although gaining custody is the most pressing immediate concern of the parents of abducted children, there are a whole range of other issues that need to be addressed. According to Paul and Walker in the following viewpoint, mediation provides the best avenue for resolving a broad array of topics that need to be settled for a satisfactory result.

Christoph C. Paul and Jamie Walker, "An International Mediation: From Child Abduction to Property Distribution," *American Journal of Family Law*, vol. 23, no. 3, Fall 2009, pp. 167–73. Copyright © 2009 Aspen Publishers, Inc. Reproduced by permission of Aspen Publishers.

As you read, consider the following questions:

1. In the fourth mediation session described in the viewpoint, what were some of the additional concerns of the parents involved that were eventually incorporated into their agreements?

2. Six months after the mediation process, the mediators had communication with the parents. What did they learn about the status of the agreement?

3. In the opinion of the authors, why was it helpful that the mediation described in the viewpoint took place prior to the filing of Hague Convention proceedings?

Offering mediation in cases of international child abduction has become standard procedure in Germany—recommended by the courts, the central authority (Federal Justice Agency), the International Social Welfare Service and others involved. For many years, there has been a network of mediators, who offer their professional assistance in such proceedings. The mediators operate according to the Breslau Declaration, *i.e.*, in the German-American case described in this [viewpoint], an American mediator (female) with a professional education background works with a German mediator (male) with a professional legal background.

The initial concern of parents of abducted children is first and foremost the question of the children's future residence: Should the child or children stay with the abducting parent or be returned to the left-behind parent? At the same time, it is also important to ask how the contacts to the other parent, to the other parent's family, to the other culture, etc., can be arranged. The range of issues the parties decide to focus on at the beginning of the mediation soon reveals that there are many more questions at stake which must at least be raised and partially—if not completely—solved during the mediation in order to find the basis for a sustainable arrangement.

In fact, this is the particular advantage of mediation. In other words, the procedure is not limited to the issues under legal dispute, but rather open to a much wider range of topics the participants need to settle.

We would like to illustrate this point by describing a German-American child abduction case we mediated recently.

Adam Between Los Angeles and Berlin

Adam, the son of Heidi and Sebastian (both in their mid-thirties), is two years old.

Heidi comes from Berlin and initially went to the United States for a year in 1994. In LA [Los Angeles], she met Sebastian and ended up staying because of him. In 1995, the two of them got married and in 1996 they bought a house. In November 2004 their son Adam was born. While Heidi had managed to work her way up the career ladder to a responsible position at a large German company, Sebastian had not yet found his calling. After four months' maternity leave, Heidi went back to work, while Sebastian took responsibility for the household and child. Starting in May 2005 Adam attended nursery school; several months later Sebastian began his training as a nurse and Heidi worked nights at home. A marriage crisis developed when Sebastian had an affair and moved out of their house in May 2006. Adam stayed with Heidi and the parents verbally agreed to take care of him alternately on a 3-month rotation basis.

In October 2006, Heidi travelled with Adam to Berlin to spend four months with her parents, where, shortly after, Sebastian came to visit her. Without informing Sebastian, Heidi agreed with her company that she would work from Berlin in the future and set up house in her own apartment near her parents. Adam began attending a German nursery school. At the beginning of December, Heidi applied for a divorce and withdrew $52,000 from a joint account. Sebastian felt completely overwhelmed by these events and sought information on the Hague Convention [on the Civil Aspects of International Child Abduction] proceedings. On a Sunday morning at the beginning of January 2007, he turned up at Heidi's door unannounced, demanding to see his son. She was too afraid to comply with his wish so he came back accompanied by the police.

Heidi was not happy in LA. She was homesick and badly missed her family. Facing the end of her marriage, she wanted to live in Berlin with her son, especially because there she could count on her family's full support. She mistrusted Sebastian and was afraid that he might return to the United States with Adam without her permission. From October onwards, her relationship to Sebastian worsened—she felt stressed by his erratic moods, by his accusations and by his threats. She did not want Adam to be pushed back and forth between his parents and their home countries; rather, she wanted him to feel at home in one place. Adam had settled in quite well and was enjoying spending time with his grandmother.

Sebastian felt guilty about having cheated on Heidi and let her down. At the same time, he did not want to lose his son. He expected to finish his training within a few months, at which point he wanted to take his share of the responsibility for raising Adam. He had applied for joint custody and demanded Heidi's return to LA together with Adam. He had no idea of Heidi's intentions: He accused her of not talking to him about her plans and trying to prevent any contact between him and Adam. Sebastian missed his son very much. He felt a complete stranger in Germany, had no confidence in the German authorities, and was bent on filing Hague Convention proceedings to enforce legally his son's repatriation to the US if necessary.

In the first week of January 2007, the German lawyers of both parents sought information on the possibility of mediation. At the beginning of the second week of January, Heidi urgently requested immediate support from the mediators. Sebastian was scheduled to return to LA the following Sunday.

From the Beginning of Mediation to an Intermediate Agreement

The first three mediation sessions took place on three consecutive days immediately after the initial contact with the mediators. After a first discussion which was held jointly, we conducted separate sessions, first with Heidi and then with Sebastian. Heidi had been well advised by her lawyer: She knew that a family court would most probably order Adam's repatriation to the United States. The idea of Adam returning to LA without her was inconceivable—but at this point so was the idea of returning to the United States. Full of despair, she described what a separation from her parents in Berlin would mean for her and for Adam's grandparents, who had built a loving relationship with their grandson. Sebastian, however, described his anger and the unbearable situation imposed upon him by Heidi. He was particularly upset by the fact that he had had to request police support to see his son to whom he had devoted such intense care. At the end of the two separate sessions, both parents said independently of each other that the mediation process should primarily deal with the principal question of where Adam was going to live in the future and how his contact with the other parent could be arranged. In the course of a first brainstorming of possible solutions the following ideas were brought forward: Adam lives in Berlin with his mother; Adam lives in LA with his father; Adam rotates between his parents (*i.e.*, he changes his residence every few months); the parents jointly move to a third country. It was quite eye-opening for the parents to imagine such (extreme) possibilities.

Subsequently, we as mediators gave the parents the opportunity to reflect upon the good and bad times of their marriage (or, respectively, their living together) as well as the time during their separation. Both described their relationship to their son and it became clear that Adam had a very good relationship to his American father and to his German mother. Supported by the mediators, both parents were able to appreciate each other in their parental roles.

In view of his impending departure, Sebastian wanted to spend as much time as possible with his son. As Heidi became aware that the contacts between Adam and his father could lead to a significant easing of tension, she agreed to arrange visits. At the same time, Sebastian became aware of Adam's strong attachment to Heidi's family. We pointed out the grandparents' importance for Adam—a fact which would have to be considered in any parental decision. The parents agreed on exact times and conditions for the meetings between father and son until the next mediation session.

At the end of the first session, we gave both parents the "assignment" to collect any further issues which should be discussed in the course of the mediation, and to seek advice from their lawyers respectively.

The Second Session

At the start of the session, Sebastian and Heidi—first separately, then jointly—reported on the contacts between father and son; Sebastian had spent several hours with Adam and enjoyed relating the experience of reconnecting with his son. The general mood during mediation was relaxed, and we asked if the parties had come up with additional issues. At the flip-chart, we jointly made a list of all topics with regard to the separation and divorce as requested by both parents, as well as questions concerning the practical implementation of joint parental custody for Adam and settlement of any proprietary issues.

The wide range of issues illustrated the fact that the parents were not only concerned with the question of Adam's future residence. Aside from this, both parents considered themselves responsible and wished to use the mediation process to reach a comprehensive settlement of their affairs. At the same time, however, it became obvious that such a far-reaching "program" could not be tackled in the three mediation sessions initially agreed upon. We asked both of them to call their lawyers prior to the next session, so that a first intermediate agreement could possibly be reached in the third session.

The Third Session

Once again, Sebastian had extensively used the opportunity to spend time with Adam. Both parents reported on a joint "family excursion" the day before, and the atmosphere was quite relaxed. We reminded both of them that no final decisions would have to be made immediately. Sebastian knew from his lawyer that he could still file a Hague Convention application at a later stage. We agreed to continue the mediation during Sebastian's next visit to Berlin in three weeks. . . .

The Fourth Session

Sebastian came to the mediation session full of confidence—he had seen Adam on the morning prior to the session and had experienced that Heidi had kept her promises.

Heidi, however, was desperate at the beginning of this fourth session. Although she had been able to arrange the professional aspects with regard to her return to the United States, she still found the idea of leaving her family in Germany inconceivable. In tears she described that she did not know how to convey to her family the inevitable decision to return to LA. Once again, both parents were given the opportunity to describe their interests, which provided the common ground for the final decision that Heidi would return to the United States with Adam.

After this piece of hard work, we began to address the other issues in the intermediate agreement. Some of them could be resolved quickly and easily, while others needed more time and further consultations with the lawyers. Some of the difficult issues were how to make arrangements for Adam in the event of the death of a parent and the principal valuation of the joint assets. Another tricky issue was which date to use to determine the final assets owned by a spouse at the end of the statutory (matrimonial) property regime: the one used under German law (the delivery of the divorce application) or the one under California law (the day of final separation). Both parents wanted to consult their lawyers by telephone once again before the next session on the following day.

The Fifth Session

Heidi reported on the discussion with her parents, on their tears at the thought of seeing their daughter and grandson move so far away again. Sebastian was relieved to realize that an amicable solution was in sight, and was prepared to meet Heidi halfway with regard to the property questions. We jointly worked out criteria for fair arrangements. Parallel interests became apparent, especially with regard to Adam's education; both parents wanted to support each other in their parental roles. As far as the distribution of assets was concerned both parties—having consulted their lawyers—settled on the valuation of assets as fixed on the day of the final separation as fair (*i.e.*, they decided to apply California law).

Working jointly with the parties, we wrote the final mediation agreement straight into the laptop. Both parents suggested practicable formulations which we as mediators examined critically before the final formulation was reached.

This last session lasted seven hours, interrupted by brief individual sessions during which Heidi and Sebastian were given the opportunity to articulate any reservations, anxieties or fears. At the end of this session, we drew up a final agreement which both parents wanted to sign. . . .

Before the agreement was signed, we asked that the lawyers again be consulted. Heidi and Sebastian decided to forgo the clause about the legal status of the agreement as they felt they had already secured legal protection. The agreement was printed out and—upon Heidi's and Sebastian's explicit request—was signed by both parents and by us as mediators.

Cooperating Instead of Fighting Led to a Good Result

About six months after the end of mediation we received an e-mail from Heidi asking what they would have to do in order to change the arrangement for the following Christmas. In the course of the ensuing correspondence with Heidi and Sebastian we learned that both of them had fully implemented the final agreement: They had divorced, the assets had been distributed and all the arrangements made with regard to Adam had been put into practice as planned.

In the course of mediation, the integration of additional issues such as the distribution of assets turned out to be quite helpful. Aside from the principal questions regarding their son, Sebastian and Heidi were able to negotiate the relevant issues needed to constitute a comprehensive and fair agreement. Such an agreement, however, was only possible with the sound counsel provided by the legal advisors in the United States and Germany, who actively supported the mediation process.

The fact that the mediation took place *prior* to the possible filing of Hague Convention proceedings and at the parents' explicit request proved to be a definite advantage. On the one hand, the situation was threatening enough to put the parents under pressure to act; on the other hand, it had not escalated to a degree which would have made any joint solution inconceivable. So, it was possible within a short period of time to create an atmosphere in which the parties—instead of fighting against each other—cooperated constructively in order to work out well-balanced and realistic solutions for the problems at hand.

> "The Hague Convention must be enforced and international law respected, not just for the sake of judicial proceedings, but for the sake of children who find themselves tangled up in an international struggle that they do not understand."

The Hague Convention Needs to Be Strengthened to Address International Child Abduction

Lindsey Douthit

Lindsey Douthit is a congressional liaison at Concerned Women for America.

In the following viewpoint, Douthit relates the well-publicized case of David Goldman, a New Jersey man whose son was abducted to Brazil by his wife, and who spent more than five years trying to regain his child. Although both the United States and Brazil had signed the Hague Convention on the Civil Aspects of International Child Abduction, many signatory countries, including Brazil in the Goldman case, refuse to enforce the convention. While the Hague Convention is a good first step, Douthit

Lindsey Douthit, "Kidnapped by Mom or Dad: American Children Abducted, Held in Foreign Countries, and Denied Access to the Other Parent," Concerned Women for America, December 21, 2009. Reproduced by permission.

contends the United States must initiate legislation that allows the government to have more authority in enforcing it.

As you read, consider the following questions:

1. Under the terms of the Hague Convention, what must occur when children are abducted to another country from their country of origin?

2. How many American children are being held captive in foreign countries?

3. What countries are the worst violators of the Hague Convention, with the most kidnappings?

When marriages end in divorce, the process is an ugly and painful one. In cases where children are involved, custody battles are often heart-wrenching and complicated. Imagine, then, that the custody battle takes place not just between two ex-spouses, but between two different countries.

David Goldman Was Separated from Son for More than Five Years

On December 2, 2009, David Goldman prepared to deliver his testimony to the bipartisan Tom Lantos Human Rights Commission. Dressed in a crisp suit and seated behind a microphone in front of a packed congressional hearing room, he looked like many other panelists who frequent Capitol Hill. However, David's personal experiences have turned him into somewhat of a celebrity, a national symbol of the neglected issue of American children abducted to foreign countries by one parent.

In June 2004, David drove his wife and their son Sean from their home in New Jersey to the airport for what she said would be a two-week vacation with her parents in her native Brazil. He waved goodbye, having no idea that it would be the last time he'd ever see his wife and that he would not see his son for four years. Once she was in Brazil, she called David to tell him that their marriage was "over" and that she had filed custody papers for Sean in the Brazilian courts. He was instructed to surrender his role as parent, never try to file for custody in the U.S. court system, and not try to divorce her to jeopardize her U.S. citizenship.

David refused to give up his parental rights and was immediately heartened to learn that both the U.S. and Brazil were signatories of the 1980 ... Hague Convention on the Civil Aspects of International Child Abduction. Under the convention, children who are abducted to another country from their country of origin and who meet the criteria under the agreement must be returned within six weeks. David's case met all of the criteria, and the courts ordered that Sean be returned to the U.S. immediately.

The story, however, was just beginning. The [Hague] Convention is not enforced by member countries, and David's wife dragged the case out through a series of appeals. She even remarried, to a Brazilian lawyer who helped stall the legal proceedings. Then she died suddenly, leaving her son in the custody of his stepfather who was described by court psychologists as inflicting emotional abuse on Sean. Even after the death of his wife, David still found his parental rights denied by the courts. To this day, he continues to fight for the return of his son.

Unfortunately, David and Sean Goldman are not the only example of American children who are abducted by one parent and held captive in a foreign country. According to the Tom Lantos Human Rights Commission, there are approximately 2,800 American children trapped in both Hague and non-Hague member countries. Japan is the world's leading kidnapper (and is not a signatory to the convention), with Mexico and India also topping the list.

According to David Goldman, Brazil currently harbors about 66 American children in blatant violation of the Hague Convention and, like Japan, has never returned an abducted American child.

Other panelists at the hearing gave testimonies of their children being taken by one parent to another country and finding themselves stripped of their parental rights, spending hundreds of thousands of dollars in legal costs, and being victims of a system in which international law is not enforced. Tom Sylvester, whose wife abducted their daughter to her native Austria, estimated that he has spent over $500,000 in legal fees and traveling to and from Austria, not to mention the toll his situation has taken on his professional life. All of the panelists present at the hearing spoke of the anguish of not only being abandoned by their spouses, but also losing their children and being stripped of their parental rights.

The Hague Convention Must Be Enforced

To try to tackle the problem of one parent abducting a U.S.-born child to another country, Representative Chris Smith (R-New Jersey) introduced H.R. 3240, legislation that would give the U.S. government greater powers in ensuring that other countries comply with the Hague Convention. As well, in an October 2009 joint statement, the U.S. joined seven other countries with children abducted to Japan—Australia, Canada, France, Italy, New Zealand, Spain, and the United Kingdom—to urge Japan to take action on open abduction cases.

Panelists at the hearing also urged the U.S. State Department and the media to bring more attention to this issue and pressure foreign governments to enforce the law. On December 7, 2009, Fox News interviewed Michael McCarty, whose wife abducted their son Liam to her native Italy. The Italian courts declared her an unfit mother, but instead of returning Liam to his homeland as a U.S. citizen, the child was placed into an Italian orphanage. During his interview, Michael urged

The Hague Abduction Convention

Does the Hague Abduction Convention Apply to My Case?

YES: Your child was abducted to a country that is a party to the Hague Convention; and Your child is younger than 16 years old;

NO: Your child was abducted to a country that is not a party to the Hague Convention; or Your child is older than 16 years old;

Background Information

For left-behind parents seeking the return of their children, one of the biggest sources of frustration is that courts in many other countries do not take into account the prior decisions made by courts in the United States. . . . When confronting this challenge, keep in mind the following three things:

Each country is a sovereign nation. . . . ;

Generally every country only has jurisdiction within its own territory and over people present within its borders; and

Although court orders from other countries may be recognized in the United States under the Uniform Child Custody Jurisdiction and Enforcement Act (UCCJEA), this is rarely true in reverse—*U.S. court orders are not generally recognized in other countries.*

In part because of these difficulties, twenty-three nations agreed to draft a treaty about international parental child abduction. . . . Between 1976 and 1980, the United States was a major force in preparing and negotiating the 1980 Hague Convention on the Civil Aspects of International Child Abduction. And on July 1, 1988, the Convention came into force for the United States.

U.S. Department of State,
"Possible Solutions: Using the Hague Abduction Convention,"
http://travel.state.gov.

Americans to write to Secretary of State [Hillary] Clinton, asking her to get directly involved in holding other governments accountable for returning abducted American children.

As members at the hearing concluded, the Hague Convention is a good start to protecting American children from being abducted and simultaneously losing their homeland and "left behind" parent, but it must be given "teeth". It is important for legislation to be passed that will give the U.S. government more authority in ensuring enforcement of the Hague Convention, for high-profile diplomats and politicians to broach the subject of abductions with their counterparts, and for the media to cast light on the countries that violate international law.

The issue of international child abductions is indeed gaining media attention and, subsequently, more traction in the public arena. On December 18, the show *20/20* featured Michael McCarty and others who faced losing their children in the web of international law and custody battles. McCarty finds himself at step one again, unfortunately—after the Italian courts declared that Liam should be placed in a neutral environment (an orphanage) and slowly rebuild his relationship with his father, McCarty's ex-wife re-abducted Liam and is now in hiding somewhere in Italy. McCarty wearily vowed that he would continue the search for his son.

Courts Tend to Favor Their Own Citizens

In the case of David and Sean Goldman, the Brazilian courts announced in [2009] that Sean should be returned to his father. However, David's ex-wife's family is once again using legal tactics to stall the ruling and prevent Sean from returning to the U.S. David is awaiting another ruling from the Brazilian Supreme Court that could come just before Christmas. His situation displays a classic symptom of one problem with the Hague Convention, that the courts in the country where the child is abducted issues the rulings. The courts tend to favor their own citizens, and therefore many recommend that the convention be amended to allow the country from which the child is taken to make custody rulings. In David's case, the [Brazilian] courts naturally favor Sean's [Brazilian] side of the family, although he was born in the U.S. and is a citizen.

The issue of international child abductions, sadly, takes the pain of broken relationships and agony of children being torn between both parents to a different level. The battle is waged not just between the couple getting divorced, but between the court systems of two different countries with different cultures and different legal standards. Victims like David Goldman and Michael McCarty continue to advocate for legislation that will give the U.S. government tools to get abducted children back and force countries to honor the law. The Hague Convention must be enforced and international law respected, not just for the sake of judicial proceedings, but for the sake of children who find themselves tangled up in an international struggle that they do not understand.

> "Despite arguments that the Hague Convention has weaknesses and can be further improved, it is still required to secure the return of children."

Despite Weaknesses, the Hague Convention Plays an Important Role in Resolving International Child Abduction

Debbie S.L. Ong

Debbie S.L. Ong is an associate professor in the law faculty at the National University of Singapore.

Singapore is not a member of the Hague Convention on the Civil Aspects of International Child Abduction, which provides specific guidelines in the cases of international child abduction. In the following viewpoint, Ong traces twenty-six cases of parental child abduction, from January 2001 to September 2006, reported to the Singapore Family Court Registry. Ten of these cases were resolved and sixteen were not. The author concludes that

Debbie S.L. Ong, "Parental Child Abduction in Singapore: The Experience of a Non-Convention Country," *International Journal of Law, Policy and the Family*, vol. 21, 2007. Copyright © 2007 Oxford University Press. Reproduced by permission of the publisher and the author.

the protections of the Hague Convention are important in securing the return of the child and that Singapore should become a signatory to the convention.

As you read, consider the following questions:

1. In the Singapore cases that were resolved, the author states the resolutions can be grouped into three categories. What are these categories?

2. What is contributing to the increased risk of parental child abductions to countries neighboring Singapore?

3. Without the protection of the Hague Convention, what are the three avenues open to the left-behind parent, according to the author?

Nearly a decade ago, Singapore was close to acceding to the Hague Convention on the Civil Aspects of International Child Abduction (Hague Convention). The *Straits Times*, the main English language newspaper in Singapore, reported on 27 October, 1997:

> The Ministry of Foreign Affairs (MFA) is considering signing the Hague Convention on the Civil Aspects of International Child Abduction. . . . It said it was working with various agencies to join the convention. It said it viewed cases of child abduction as 'very personal and private in nature and difficult to resolve between the two parties'. But where the ministry could intervene officially, based on diplomatic goodwill with other countries, it would do so. It said it had helped in a number of cases but was unable to release statistics, as these were confidential matters.

However, to date, Singapore has not acceded to the Hague Convention and is presently not a party to this international treaty. It is understood that the case for accession to the Hague Convention is still open, nearly a decade after serious first consideration.

Research Presented on Parental Child Abduction in Singapore

This [viewpoint] presents data and analyses on unpublished cases and materials from the SFCR [Singapore Family Court Registry] from January 2001 to September 2006. It gives a snapshot of the number and characteristics of parental child abduction cases recorded in court proceedings including the ways in which the disputes are resolved (or unresolved) without the machinery of the Hague Convention. It does not attempt to represent a comprehensive collection of all instances of child abduction; instead, it gives an exploratory picture of the landscape on this issue. This [viewpoint] also discusses the welfare principle in the context of international parental child abduction as well as how a non-Convention country can still cooperate in the elimination of such abduction by the use of the principle. It is hoped that the data presented in this [viewpoint] will be of value to Singapore's current Ministry of Community Development, Youth and Sports, which continues to study the case for Singapore's participation as a Convention country.

Research reveals that 26 cases of parental child abduction have come to the attention of the SFCR in the past five years. Clearly there are other instances of child abduction that are not recorded formally in court proceedings. For example, there are those which may come to public attention through the media but where no proceedings are sought in the courts. . . .

In the research which yielded 26 cases, there were 22 cases involving outbound abductions where children were allegedly removed from Singapore. Only four inbound cases of abduction into Singapore were found. Of the 26 cases, ten were resolved in that the files record the return of the child to the country of residence from which she was removed. Sixteen cases remained unresolved in that the files do not contain records of the child's return. . . .

As Singapore has not acceded to the Hague Convention on the Civil Aspects of International Child Abduction, the cases are not resolved within the mechanism of the Convention. In the cases where the child is returned to the country of residence, we observe broadly three groups of cases marking the circumstances of return. The ten cases, described in varying degrees of detail, which involved the return of the child, may be placed into the following broad categories for the purposes of analysis.

16 Unresolved Cases

In the more dramatic of the cases, the children were 're-abducted' to the country of residence by the other parent....

Another cluster of cases demonstrates that in some cases, the abducting parent is willing to abide by court orders made in the country *to which the child is abducted*. In such cases, if the court employs the principles of the Hague Convention and generally orders the summary return of the child to the place of residence, it is able, to a limited extent, to extend the benefits of the Hague Convention to the aggrieved parent.

In [another] cluster of cases, the abductor mothers had understandable reasons for leaving the jurisdiction, the driving force seeming to be for reasons other than preventing the left-behind spouse from having contact with the child. The return of the children did not seem difficult to secure. These parents removed the children out of Singapore for a few months before returning them and had the matter resolved by the Singapore court....

In 16 of the cases, there was no record in the files of the child being returned to the place of residence. In some of these cases, the parties try to seek assistance from the police and diplomatic channels through the Ministry of Foreign Affairs....

Goals of the Hague Convention

[The] Hague Convention [on the Civil Aspects of International Child Abduction] gives priority to children remaining with their biological parents or relatives or with nonrelatives in the country of origin and to protection of children from child abduction, selling, or trafficking. At the same time, it contains language emphasizing the benefits to children of a caring family environment, of intercountry adoption when suitable placement in the country of origin is not possible, and of considering children's best interests.

Leslie Doty Hollingsworth,
"Does the Hague Convention on Intercountry Adoption
Address the Protection of Adoptees' Cultural Identity?
And Should It?" Social Work, *October 2008.*

There Are More Outbound than Inbound Abductions

The highest number of abductions involved China (five cases), followed by Australia (three cases). Two cases each were found in the neighbouring countries Vietnam, Thailand and Indonesia as well as the US and UK [United Kingdom]. Of these, Australia, Thailand, the US and UK are Contracting States while Vietnam and Indonesia are not. Mainland China itself is not a party to the Convention.

The recent trend of the rising number of marriages between Singaporeans and spouses from the region points toward the increased risk of parental child abduction involving the neighbouring countries. The increasing number of Singaporeans marrying foreigners, particular those from China and Vietnam have been recently highlighted:

Last year (i.e., 2005), 6529 male Singaporeans and permanent residents married foreign brides, the highest number in ten years, according to the Department of Statistics. The number is up from 5210 the previous year and 4425 in 2003. This means one in four Singapore men who got married last year tied the knot with foreigners. The real figure may be higher; as some men marry overseas. . . . The *Straits Times* understands Malaysians still form the bulk of foreign brides, but Vietnamese and Chinese brides are gaining ground.

There were 22 cases of outward bound abduction cases, which is more than five times the number of inbound abductions. This can partially be explained by the small size of Singapore. With a physical land area of less than 700 square kilometres, the resulting social interconnectedness in Singapore leaves less room for a parent to hide a child. Based on these data, if Singapore accedes to the Convention, parents resident in Singapore stand to benefit much from it, since there is likely to be more outbound abductions than inbound ones. But even if this were not so, in a world that is so interconnected and interdependent today, Singapore can protect its children only if it also extends reciprocal assistance to foreign children abducted to Singapore.

In the majority of cases resolved, the abductor parent participated in the court proceedings and was willing to reach an agreement or abide by the court order made in either country. The cluster of cases described earlier where the abductor mothers returned to Singapore for resolution reveals that these mothers had explicable reasons for leaving the jurisdiction: one was apparently suffering domestic abuse, another was remarried to her husband who lived outside Singapore. However, without such submission to the court's jurisdiction or in cases where the abductor parent and/or child cannot be located, this route of resolution is not available. In such cases, self-help seems the only alternative. Two of the ten cases depended on the left-behind parent's re-abduction of the child, which requires tremendous resources of time, effort and money. The hiring of a private investigator to track the child in a foreign country is usually far too costly for most parents. In two of the *unresolved* cases, there were various unsuccessful attempts by the left-behind parent to seek assistance from the police and diplomatic channels. This shows that little aid can be obtained from these avenues. The state's assistance can be guaranteed only by international treaties such as the Hague Convention. . . .

A Case for the Hague Convention in Singapore

Despite arguments that the Hague Convention has weaknesses and can be further improved, it is still required to secure the return of children. In Singapore's experience, without the state's guarantee of assistance and the reciprocal resources of other contracting states, the left-behind parent can depend on only three avenues: re-abduction through use of personal re-sources, submission of abductor-parent to jurisdiction of court in either country and, finally, informal diplomatic channels and assistance from the departments of police and immigration and control. The first is extremely costly and largely an impossible avenue, the second depends on the abductor-parent's strategies, and the last has proven ineffective.

As a non-Convention country, there is no assurance that a foreign court applying the welfare principle will order the summary return of a child wrongfully removed from Singapore. In England, its highest court has stated unequivocally that the policies of the Hague Convention are not relevant in cases involving non-Convention countries.

The case for Singapore to become a party to the Convention has been argued with reference to her commitment to the Convention on the Rights of the Child (CRC). By becoming a signatory to the CRC, Singapore has by Article 11, 'committed to take measures to combat the illicit transfer and non-return of children abroad' and '[t]o this end, [to] promote the conclusion of bilateral or multilateral agreements or accession to existing agreements'. It is not unreasonable to suggest from this commitment that Singapore may be required to take greater steps to engage in any international move(s) to ensure the protection of children from the 'modern' ill of their own parental abduction of them.

"The case illustrates the complexities of adopting children in a poor country with few working government institutions and a corrupt bureaucracy."

Missionaries Operated with Good Intentions in Rescuing Haitian Children for Adoption

Joel Millman and Jeffrey Ball

Joel Millman and Jeffrey Ball are reporters for the Wall Street Journal.

Following the devastating earthquake in Haiti on January 12, 2010, a missionary group from Idaho, the New Life Children's Refuge, took thirty-three Haitian children to the Dominican Republic, where they planned to build an orphanage. The Haitian government charged the missionaries with illegal abduction, jailed them, and on May 17, 2010, freed the last missionary. In the following viewpoint, the authors report that the claims of the Haitian government are at odds with statements from the families of the children who claim that they provided written permission to the missionaries to take their children. Despite this, the

Joel Millman and Jeffrey Ball, "Haitians, Parents Defend Arrested Americans," *Wall Street Journal*, February 5, 2010. Reprinted by permission of The Wall Street Journal, copyright © 2010 Dow Jones & Company, Inc. All Rights Reserved Worldwide. License number 2499450537819.

missionaries can be faulted for a failure of due diligence—in at least three cases, the letters were from people who weren't the birth parents of the children, maintain the authors.

As you read, consider the following questions:

1. What facts do the authors provide to support their contention that the missionaries failed to exercise proper due diligence in taking the children?

2. What is the family situation of most children in Haitian orphanages, according to the authors?

3. What did the Idaho missionaries promise the parents that was an inducement for them to give up their children?

The Haitian government is accusing Laura Silsby and nine other American missionaries with illegally abducting 33 children, most of them from the small town of Callebasse, in the mountains south of the capital.

Two Sides to Haitian Story

But some of the children's own families and friends here disagree. On Friday [in February 2010], some said they willingly handed over the children, want the Americans freed, and want them to continue with plans to have the children live in an orphanage in the Dominican Republic.

The account from Callebasse stands in contrast to the image portrayed by the Haitian government of Ms. Silsby and the other missionaries. On Thursday, a Haitian judge charged the ten U.S. citizens with abduction and conspiracy, charges that could land them in jail for years.

But the message from the town where 20 of the 33 children were taken is consistent with the message from Ms. Silsby's own family and friends. Adonna Sander, Ms. Silsby's mother, said Thursday night that her daughter's group had written permission from the children's parents to take them.

Despite the villagers' support for Ms. Silsby's efforts, their accounts of her visit revealed details that raised questions over her attempts at due diligence.

At least three people who agreed to send their children weren't their birth parents. Milien Brutus, 28, the brother of one nine-year-old boy, authorized passage with the Idaho group, as did Melanie Augustin, 57, who agreed to send a girl she adopted as an infant, nine-year-old Loudinie Jovene. Natanya Geffraid, a 24-year-old woman with no children of her own, signed off on sending a child to whom she said she is godmother.

The Idaho group also promised to bring the Callebasse villagers to visit the children next year in the Dominican Republic.

"They said we would all go in a bus together," said Ms. Augustin. She added that acquiring a Haitian passport was beyond the means of anyone in Callebasse, citing a price of 1,000 Haitian dollars, or US$125. The villagers said no one from the government had come yet to talk to them about what happened.

On Friday night, families of the detained Americans released a statement saying they would continue to seek their relatives' release.

Complex Issues Illustrated

The case illustrates the complexities of adopting children in a poor country with few working government institutions and a corrupt bureaucracy. Most children in Haitian orphanages aren't orphans, but have been put there by desperately poor families that hope they will be better fed and educated.

At the same time, there are many cases of Haitian children being trafficked for forced labor or sex, and the Haitian government says it must enforce regulations for adoptions strictly to avoid such situations. It is worried that the recent earthquake will lead to more trafficking.

Haiti's Motives Questioned

"Haiti's decision to prosecute the Baptist missionaries may be motivated, in part, by the need to show its own people and the world that it is a viable entity that is tackling the grave problem of international child abductions in Haiti," Christopher J. Schmidt, a lawyer with Bryan Cave L.L.P. in St. Louis who has been involved in multiple cases of international kidnapping, said in a statement.

Marc Lacey,
"Haiti Charges Americans with Child Abduction,"
New York Times, *February 4, 2010.*

Haiti has a long tradition of families handing over their children. Some villagers here considered the Jan. 28 arrival of Ms. Silsby and an Idaho church group "a miracle," and a blessing from God.

"I wanted my son to be another person. I didn't want him to have the life I have," said Jean Anchello Cantave, 36, who gave a five-year-old son, Ancito, to the Americans. He loaded a second child, three-year-old Magdaline, onto the bus, too, he said.

"But she cried so much, I took her back," Mr. Cantave said.

Pointing to a small square of brown earth behind his whitewashed stucco home, Mr. Cantave explained his own wealth was only what he can raise from the dirt—in this season, the carrots and cabbages he will try to sell at a nearby street market. He said he considered the chance to send two of his three children off to school no less than winning a lottery.

"The chance to educate a child is a chance for an entire family to prosper," he said, as neighbors—many of whom also sent children with the Idaho church group—nodded in agreement. To the question, what kinds of adults might these educated children become, they shouted: "nurse," "doctor," "airplane pilot," "mechanic," "plumber" and "someone with a job in an office."

Ms. Silsby's family in Idaho described her as following a family tradition of missionary work helping the poor. "Laura was raised in a missionary's home and just felt the burden for mission work," her father, John Sander, said Friday, speaking in the modest building that houses his denture-making practice on a residential street in Twin Falls.

Ms. Silsby's father said it was typical of his daughter to help out people she thought were in need. "She's always been very helpful to help people if they need a place to stay," he said.

Steve McMullen, a longtime friend of the Sander family in Idaho, said he spoke by phone to Ms. Silsby while she was in the Dominican Republic, and that during the call she said she was in a government office registering the names of the children her group was intending to bring back into the country from Haiti.

But the plans went awry. Sitting in his Twin Falls office, Mr. Sander shook his head. "I don't know," he said. "We better pray for a miracle."

> "The sentiment behind intercountry adoption may sound noble and often is. . . . But intercountry adoptions happen in a fuzzy and sometimes murky world. One worry is that demand creates supply."

Missionaries Took Haitian Children Who Weren't Orphans into Custody

Economist

The Economist *is a London-based weekly newspaper dealing with international affairs.*

Members of the New Life Children's Refuge, Christian missionaries from Idaho, were arrested in Haiti after the group attempted to rescue thirty-three Haitian children from the aftermath of the January 2010 earthquake. The missionaries were taking the children to the Dominican Republic to place them in an orphanage. However, they failed to fill out any paperwork, and it turned out that many of the children had families. This high-profile case illustrates several problems associated with intercountry adoptions, according to the author. The author fur-

Economist "Saviours or Kidnappers?" vol. 394, February 6, 2010, pp. 66–67. Copyright © The Economist Newspaper Limited, London 2010. All rights reserved. Reproduced by permission.

ther asserts that while intercountry adoptions sound good in theory, they do nothing to address the underlying issues of poverty and abuse in the poor countries that supply most children.

As you read, consider the following questions:

1. What other example of alleged kidnapping of children does the author cite?

2. What are some of the issues with intercountry adoptions that the author explains?

3. What are some of the experiences of Romania that critics of intercountry adoption point to in support of their position?

It must have seemed like a good idea at the time. The New Life Children's Refuge, a Christian group from Idaho, saw no need to bother with paperwork or official permission when they decided to take 33 Haitian children to the Dominican Republic where they apparently hoped to build an orphanage.

Furious officials arrested ten of the group's members on charges of kidnapping (which they deny). Many of the children turned out to have families. A similar row erupted in 2007 when workers from Zoé's Ark, a French charity, were accused of kidnapping 103 children in Chad [in central Africa]. Ostensibly orphans from the Darfur region of Sudan, destined for adoption in France, many turned out to be local children, and not orphans. Six charity workers were jailed.

Issues Around Intercountry Adoptions Are Complex

The sentiment behind intercountry adoption may sound noble and often is. Why should governments stand between loving people in one country and needy children in another? Support for intercountry adoption is particularly strong in America, where parents adopt more foreign children than all the rest of the world. Some would-be adopters may at times be overhasty but Michele Bond, the senior State Department official dealing with the issue, insists that those concerned act from the best possible motives.

But intercountry adoptions happen in a fuzzy and sometimes murky world. One worry is that demand creates supply. Outsiders' money can distort the decisions of officials and parents in poor countries. That may hamper chances of the most desirable outcome, in which children are fostered by relatives or adopted locally. Very few children described as orphans have no living relatives. If they move to another country, their chances of staying in touch with family members shrivel. Even the most ardent free-marketeers do not support free trade in children, with blonde female babies attracting a hefty premium.

Another worry is that adopted children may disappear from view when they cross international borders. International law stipulates that reports on the adopted child should be sent regularly to the source country. In some countries that is observed punctiliously. In others it is in effect voluntary. American law, in particular, does not require parents to send such reports. Once in America, an adopted child is treated like any other, with the state getting involved only in cases of evident abuse. Officials in countries such as Ethiopia or Ukraine may lack the means or motivation to chase up dilatory American parents.

Romania's Experience Raises Concerns

Many critics of intercountry adoption cite experiences in Romania. Following reports of scandalous conditions in orphanages there after the collapse of communism, outsiders flocked to adopt children. But of the 30,000 children adopted by foreigners between 1990 and 2000, around 20,000 are now untraceable, according to Rupert Wolfe Murray, who worked as a lobbyist on the issue.

Copyright © 2010 by Rainer Hachfeld and CagleCartoons.com. All rights reserved.

Roelie Post, who as a European Commission official dealt with adoption in the run-up to Romania's entry to the European Union, has written a book on her experience of dealing with what she sees as a powerful adoption lobby that preys on weak and poor countries. Mr. Wolfe Murray says that after wars and natural disasters adoption agencies descend like "vultures" to find suitable children. The countries that provide the most children for international adoption include China, Vietnam, Kazakhstan and, until recently, Guatemala, which are also among those with the weakest legal systems, he notes.

Most adoption agencies are nonprofit outfits that see their work as entirely charitable. They may charge only expenses and a reasonable fee, according to the Hague Convention on intercountry adoption [officially the Hague Convention on Protection of Children and Co-operation in Respect of Intercountry Adoption]. An international treaty with a supporting bureaucracy, it has had growing clout since America joined it in 2008. But the sums involved leave ample room for doubt. A

Love Beyond Borders, an agency helping would-be parents adopt children from Haiti and elsewhere, says the process may cost more than $30,000.

The Hague [Adoption Convention] rules also govern the agencies' accreditation. That should, for example, stop the practice (often criticised as exploitative) of putting photographs of "children awaiting adoption" on their Web sites. But American agencies may dodge that by saying that they are seeking accreditation, or cite some other endorsement, for example by the consulate of the country they are dealing with.

As legal regimes on adoption tighten, activity tends to shift. When Romania banned intercountry adoption, agencies moved to lightly regulated Moldova and then Ukraine. Hans van Loon, the secretary general of The Hague regulatory body, highlights Guatemala, once the source of 5,000 annual adoptions, mainly to America. That seemed a lot for a country of 13m [million] people. (Only about 10,000 foreign adoptions a year take place in China.) Now the number has dropped to zero after a temporary suspension. When it resumes, he expects only a few hundred children, mainly with disabilities, to be adopted.

Intercountry adoption may often be wonderful for the children and families concerned. But it does not solve the problems of poverty and abuse that make it so seemingly desirable.

Periodical and Internet Sources Bibliography

The following articles have been selected to supplement the diverse views presented in this chapter.

David M. Allender	"Child Abductions: Nightmares in Progress," *FBI Law Enforcement Bulletin*, July 2007.
Janet Chiancone, Linda K. Girdner, and Patricia M. Hoff	"Issues in Resolving Cases of International Child Abduction by Parents," *Juvenile Justice Bulletin*, December 2001.
Matthew Clark	"Haiti 'Orphan' Rescue Mission: Adoption or Child Trafficking?" *Christian Science Monitor*, February 1, 2010.
Commonweal	"Good Intentions?" February 26, 2010.
Samantha Henry	"International Custody Wars Abound as Abductions by Parents Rise," *Washington Post*, June 21, 2009.
Dahlia Lithwick	"All in the Family," *Slate*, January 12, 2010.
A.D. McKenzie	"Haiti: 'Adoption Not the Best Choice for Quake Orphans,'" Inter Press Service, January 23, 2010. http://ipsnews.net.
Peter Opper	"Preventing Heartbreak in Adoption: Understanding the Rights of All Parties," *American Journal of Family Law*, vol. 19, no. 3, Fall 2005.
Daniel B. Wood	"Sean Goldman Case Highlights Rising International Child Abduction," *Christian Science Monitor*, December 23, 2009.

For Further Discussion

Chapter 1

1. Joint custody arrangements have gained in popularity since California passed a law in 1980 favoring joint custody. David Levy is in favor of joint custody, while Nicki Bradley says in practice most families with joint custody are unhappy with the arrangement. What reasons does each give to support his or her position? With which position do you agree, and why?

2. The rights of gay parents in child custody cases is the subject of debate, with some offering equal custody rights to gays while others argue to limit their rights. Charlotte J. Patterson cites research to conclude there is no reason to discriminate against gays, while John W. Kennedy maintains gay individuals should not be granted custody of children. What reasons does each give to support his or her position? With which position do you agree, and why?

Chapter 2

1. Thomas D. Williams defends the refusal of Boston's Catholic Charities to allow same-sex couples to adopt children from its agency on the basis that all adoption agencies discriminate in some form or another. Maria Carmela Sioco argues that research shows that there is no scientific evidence that children are negatively impacted by being raised by gay parents. Are these arguments mutually exclusive?

2. The return of seven-year-old Artyom Savelyev to his native Russia by his adoptive U.S. mother made headlines in April 2010 and highlighted some of the issues surrounding international adoptions. Joanne Bamberger says that

returning an adopted child should never be an option. Do you agree with her perspective? Can you suggest alternatives that the adoptive mother might have considered?

Chapter 3

1. The decision by the Texas Department of Family and Protective Services to remove more than four hundred children from a fundamentalist Mormon compound because of suspected sexual abuse of minors set off a debate about the role of government in custody cases. Mary Zeiss Stange argues that religious stereotyping was inappropriately used in seizing the children, while Katy Vine worries that children were returned to a potentially dangerous environment. From the facts included in these viewpoints, do you feel the raid was justified? Should the children have been returned? Cite evidence to support your position.

2. In the United States, nearly 2 million children have parents in prison, with the number of mothers in prison increasing by more than 100 percent over the past fifteen years. Beth Schwartzapfel describes an experimental program where newborns remain with their incarcerated mothers for anywhere from one month to three years. Do you think the benefits of such a program outweigh the negatives involved in having a newborn in penal custody?

Chapter 4

1. The increase in international parental child abductions and the failure of the international legal system to return these children has led some parents to hire private individuals to recover their children through abduction. Do you condone private recovery efforts such as the one related by Nadya Labi? Why or why not? How can the "best interests of the child" be served in cases of international parental child abduction?

2. Following the January 2010 earthquake, Laura Silsby and nine other American missionaries took thirty-three children from the devastation of Haiti with the intent of placing them in an orphanage in the Dominican Republic. Many of these children turned out to already have families, and Silsby and other missionaries were arrested on charges of kidnapping. The incident was highly controversial, with such commentators as Joel Millman and Jeffrey Ball arguing that the missionaries operated with the best interests of the children in mind, while others such as the *Economist* contend that even well-intentioned efforts can have negative consequences for the children. What are some of the complications that both viewpoints cite? Do you think the missionaries were justified or not, and why?

Organizations to Contact

The editors have compiled the following list of organizations concerned with all the issues debated in this book. The descriptions are derived from materials provided by the organizations. All have publications or information available for interested readers. The names, addresses, phone and fax numbers, and e-mail and Internet addresses may change. Be aware that many organizations take several weeks or longer to respond to inquiries, so allow as much time as possible.

Center for the Study of Social Policy
1575 Eye Street NW, Suite 500, Washington, DC   20005
(202) 371-1565 • fax (202) 371-1472
e-mail: info@cssp.org
website: www.cssp.org

The Center for the Study of Social Policy was established in 1979 with the goal of providing public policy analysis and technical assistance to states and localities, in a way that blended high academic standards with direct responsiveness to the needs of policy makers and practitioners. The center's work is concentrated in the areas of family and children's services, income supports, neighborhood-based services, education reform, family support, disability and health care policy, and long-term care for the elderly.

Child Welfare League of America
1726 M Street NW, Suite 500, Washington, DC   20036
(202) 688-4200 • fax: (202) 833-1689
website: www.cwla.org

The Child Welfare League of America, a social welfare organization concerned with setting standards for welfare and human services agencies, works to improve care and services for abused, dependent, or neglected children, youth, and their families. It provides consultation and conducts research on all aspects of adoption. It publishes the bimonthly journal *Child Welfare* and several books, such as *Child Welfare: A Journal of Policy, Practice, and Program.*

Children's Rights Council
9470 Annapolis Road, Suite 310, Lanham, MD   20706
(301) 459-1220
e-mail: info@crckids.org
website: www.crckids.org

The Children's Rights Council is concerned with the healthy development of children of divorced and separated parents. Its efforts are concentrated on strengthening marriage, reforming child custody laws, minimizing hostilities between separated or divorced parents, and advocating for a child's right to grow up in a healthy family environment. The council publishes the quarterly newsletter *Speak Out for Children.*

The Fatherhood Coalition (TFC)
PO Box 310, Turners Falls, MA   01376
(617) 723-DADS
website: www.fatherhoodcoalition.org

The Fatherhood Coalition is an organization of men and women advocating the institution of fatherhood. It works to promote shared parenting and to end the discrimination and persecution faced by divorced and unwed fathers in society at large and specifically in Massachusetts. The coalition is active in the fight against the abuse of restraining orders, especially in divorce cases. The organization's website offers articles and links to other pro-fatherhood and male advocacy groups.

Institute for Adoption Information, Inc.
409 Dewey Street, Bennington, VT   05201
(802) 442-7815
e-mail: info@adoptioninformationinstitute.org
website: www.adoptioninformationinstitute.org

The Institute for Adoption Information, Inc., is a nonprofit organization of adoptees, birth parents, adoptive parents, adoption professionals, and others who have united to enhance public understanding of adoption. It develops tools used to educate others about adoption and to dispel the myths and stereotypes surrounding adoption. It publishes and distributes *An Educator's Guide to Adoption* and other writings.

Joint Council on International Children's Services (JCICS)
117 South Saint Asaph Street, Alexandria, VA   22314
(703) 535-8045 • fax: (703) 535-8049
e-mail: info@jointcouncil.org
website: www.jcics.org

The Joint Council on International Children's Services (JCICS) serves as an advocate on behalf of children needing permanent homes with caring families and promotes ethical practices in international adoption. Its website includes regularly updated links to the most recent information about adoption policies in the United States and many other countries around the world. JCICS publishes a series of Summary Reports on issues affecting international adoptions.

National Adoption Center (NAC)
1500 Walnut Street, Suite 701, Philadelphia, PA   19102
(800) TO-ADOPT
e-mail: nac@adopt.org
website: www.adopt.org

The National Adoption Center (NAC) promotes the adoption of older, disabled, and minority children and of siblings who seek to be placed together. It provides information, registration, family recruitment, and matching referral services for children and prospective adoptive parents. It publishes the semiannual *National Adoption Center Newsletter*.

National Center for Lesbian Rights (NCLR)
870 Market Street, Suite 370, San Francisco, CA   94102
(415) 392-6257 • fax: (415) 392-8442

e-mail: info@nclrights.org
website: www.nclrights.org

The National Center for Lesbian Rights (NCLR) is a lesbian, multicultural, and legal resource center that advocates lesbian rights. The center condemns sexual orientation–based discrimination in health care, the workplace, and society in general. In addition to providing counseling services, the center distributes brochures, a biannual newsletter, and the *Lesbian & Gay Parenting Bibliography*.

National Council for Adoption

225 N. Washington Street, Alexandria, VA   22314-2561
(703) 299-6633 • fax: (703) 299-6004
e-mail: ncfa@adoptioncouncil.org
website: www.adoptioncouncil.org

Representing volunteer agencies, adoptive parents, adoptees, and birth parents, the National Council for Adoption works to protect the institution of adoption and to ensure the confidentiality of all involved in the adoption process. It strives for adoption regulations that will ensure the protection of birth parents, children, and adoptive parents. Its biweekly newsletter, *Memo*, provides updates on state and federal legislative and regulatory changes affecting adoption. It also publishes the *Adoption Fact Book*.

Organization of Parents Through Surrogacy (OPTS)

PO Box 611, Gurnee, IL   60031
(847) 782-0224
e-mail: bzager@msn.com
website: www.opts.com

A national network, the Organization of Parents Through Surrogacy (OPTS) promotes the concept of parenthood through surrogate mothers. It offers information and lobbies legislatures to pass laws in support of surrogacy. OPTS publishes a periodic newsletter and maintains a listing of surrogate/parenting centers.

Bibliography of Books

Dan Amneus   *The Case for Father Custody.*
                      Alhambra, CA: Primrose Press, 2000.

Amy J.L. Baker   *Adult Children of Parental Alienation
                      Syndrome: Breaking the Ties That
                      Bind.* New York: W.W. Norton & Co.,
                      2007.

Nadir Baksh and   *In the Best Interest of the Child: A
Laurie Murphy   Manual for Divorcing Parents.*
                      Prescott, AZ: Hohm Press, 2007.

Nell Bernstein   *All Alone in the World: Children of
                      the Incarcerated.* New York: New
                      Press, 2005.

Janet Chiancone,   *Issues in Resolving Cases of
Linda Girdner,   International Child Abduction by
and Patricia Hoff   Parents.* Washington, DC: U.S.
                      Department of Justice, Office of
                      Justice Programs, Office of Juvenile
                      Justice and Delinquency Prevention,
                      2001.

Ken Connelly   *Throwing Stones: Parental Child
                      Abduction Through the Eyes of a
                      Child.* New York: iUniverse, 2009.

Richard A.   *The Parental Alienation Syndrome: A
Gardner   Guide for Mental Health and Legal
                      Professionals.* 2nd ed. Cresskill, NJ:
                      Creative Therapeutics, 1998.

Ann M.   *Handling Child Custody, Abuse, and
Haralambie   Adoption Cases.* 3rd ed. Eagan, MN:
                      Thomas Reuters/West, 2009.

Joseph Helmreich and Paul Marcus *Warring Parents, Wounded Children, and the Wretched World of Child Custody: Cautionary Tales.* Westport, CT: Praeger, 2008.

Deedra Hunter, with Tom Monte *Winning Custody: A Woman's Guide to Retaining Custody of Her Children.* New York: St. Martin's Griffin, 2001.

B.J. Jones, Mark Tilden, and Kelly Gaines-Stoner *The Indian Child Welfare Act Handbook: A Legal Guide to the Custody and Adoption of Native American Children.* 2nd ed. Chicago, IL: American Bar Association, 2008.

Craig Key *A Deadly Game of Tug of War: The Kelsey Smith-Briggs Story.* Garden City, NY: Morgan James Publishing, 2007.

Harry D. Krause and David D. Meyer *Family Law in a Nutshell.* 5th ed. St. Paul, MN: Thomson/West, 2007.

Kathryn Kuehnle and Leslie Drozd, eds. *Child Custody Litigation: Allegations of Child Sexual Abuse.* New York: Haworth Press, 2005.

Renae Lapin *School Days & the Divorce Maze: A Complete Guide for Joint Custody Parents in Managing Your Child's Successful School Career.* Hollywood, FL: Frederick Fell Publishers, 2008.

Arlene Istar Lev *The Complete Lesbian & Gay Parenting Guide.* New York: Berkley Books, 2004.

Ken Lewis   *Child Custody Evaluations by Social Workers: Understanding the Five Stages of Custody.* Washington, DC: NASW Press, 2009.

Mimi E. Lyster   *Child Custody: Building Parenting Agreements That Work.* 4th ed. Berkeley, CA: Nolo Press, 2003.

Gerald P. Mallon   *Gay Men Choosing Parenthood.* New York: Columbia University Press, 2004.

Susan Markens   *Surrogate Motherhood and the Politics of Reproduction.* Berkeley, CA: University of California Press, 2007.

Mary Ann Mason   *From Father's Property to Children's Rights: The History of Child Custody in the United States.* New York: Columbia University Press, 1994.

Mary Ann Mason   *The Custody Wars: Why Children Are Losing the Legal Battle and What We Can Do About It.* New York: Basic Books, 1999.

Brette McWhorter Sember   *Gay & Lesbian Parenting Choices: From Adopting or Using a Surrogate to Choosing the Perfect Father.* Franklin Lakes, NJ: Career Press, 2006.

Debora L. Spar   *The Baby Business: How Money, Science, and Politics Drive the Commerce of Conception.* Boston, MA: Harvard Business School Press, 2006.

Guy J. White   *Child Custody A to Z: Winning with Evidence.* New York: iUniverse, 2005.

Index

Group sex, 41

Guardianship proceedings, children's preferences, 110–111

Gupta, Vanita, 154, 156

H

Haddad, Richard, 161

Hague Convention on the Civil Aspects of International Child Abduction

Adam/mediation case, 176, 177–178, 181, 183–184

case application determination, 189

experience of Singapore, 198–199

goals of, 196

local citizen priorities, 190–191

need for enforcement, 188–190

Todd Hopson case, 162, 163, 166–167, 174

weaknesses vs. importance of, 192–199

Haitian children adoption controversy

missionaries' good intentions, 200–204

non-orphan status of children, 205–209

Hamilton, Marci, 134

Handicapped children, 72

Harrison, Michelle, 90

Hedrick, Marsha, 58

Heiligenstein, Annie, 147

Henderson Nevada Police Department, 161

Hession, Gregory A., 134

Hines, Barbara, 154, 156

HIV-AIDS, 53

Hollingsworth, Donald Robinson, 88–89

Hollingsworth, Leslie Doty, 196

Hollingsworth, Sean, 88–89

"Homosexual Parenting: Is It Time for Change" (ACP), 41

Hopson, Todd, 165–175

House of Representatives (U.S.)

immigration bill rejection, 158

SCRA, 121–124, 126–130

"How Does the Sexual Orientation of Parents Matter?" (Biblarz & Stacey), 42

H.R. 4460 amendment (SCRA), 124

Huggins, Sharon L., 34–35

I

Illegal immigrant mothers. *See* Mothers who are illegal immigrants

Immigrations and Customs Enforcement Department (ICE, Homeland Security), 155, 156–158

Imprisonment of children. *See* Children in prison (with their mothers)

"Incarcerated Mothers: Mental Health Child Welfare Policy, and the Special Concerns of Undocumented Mothers" (Johansen), 157

Indiana women's prison with children, 151

Intercountry adoption complexity, 206–207